young BOSS

by

ISABELLE GUARINO

Copyright © 2023 by Isabelle Guarino.
All rights reserved. This book or any portion thereof may not be reproduced or used in any manner whatsoever without the express written permission of the publisher except for the use of brief quotations in a book review.

Publishing Services provided by Paper Raven Books LLC
Printed in the United States of America
First Printing, 2023

Hardback ISBN 978-1-7343153-4-9
Paperback ISBN 978-1-7343153-6-3

Dedication

This book is written for my father, who was the ultimate young boss. He started his first business at fifteen and his real estate career at age eighteen. He never looked down on anyone because they were young, but instead chose to believe that everyone was capable, coachable, and worthy. I adored my father, and he taught me most of what I know about the business world. I am inspired by his legacy and have chosen to carry on his business and build more businesses in his honor. I hope to one day pass the entrepreneurship bug to my future children and carry this onto future generations. Thank you, Dad, for believing in me always. Your faith in me has changed my life forever.

"You got this." - Dad

Chapter 1
WHY, WHY, WHY

My goal in writing this book is not to instruct you on how to run your business. After all, we are probably in completely different industries. My goal is to share with you some major keys I've learned along the way to becoming a young boss. Before the age of thirty, I was named "Top Senior Housing Influencer" by *GlobeSt Magazine* and *Aging Media Network* 2020's "Future Leader" in Senior Housing, and I had built eight companies over the previous seven years. I absolutely love building and running businesses and teams. Since then, I have been named one of the "Women to Watch in Real Estate" by *Think Realty Magazine* in 2023 and one of the "Top 5 Disruptive Entrepreneurs Going into 2023" by *Dallas News*. I want to share what worked and what didn't work for me. I want to enlighten you about some positive mindsets and approaches I think can apply to almost every field. I want to talk about the struggles and joys of being a young boss in a Boomer's world. I want to cover what it's like to be a woman in a male-dominated field and how to not let being young get you down. I have the joy of hosting an incredible podcast, The YoungBoss Podcast, where I get to interview other incredible young bosses under the age of forty on what they do and how they got where they are. We talk about everything on the show! It's a great listen. If you haven't subscribed, be sure to check it out at theyoungbosspodcast.com!

Being a young boss is the best job in the world. I get to step into my leadership role and learn what to do and not do every single day. I feel honored to be an entrepreneur. Many people are terrified of working for themselves, but I wouldn't have it any other way, and my assumption is neither would you. Or maybe you picked up this book because you WANT to become a young boss, and I'm happy to have you here, too! In the world of entrepreneurship, it's important we don't go it alone. My intention is to build a family, a crew, a circle of trusted friends you can rely on when you need to throw around new business ideas or share failures, fears, and big wins! Some of your other friends may never understand the need in your soul to do something on your own. When you start winning big and the numbers you're talking about are just out of their league, you may start to shut down and feel you can't talk with them about such things. Not here! This is a group that wants to push you, a community that wants to be by your side during the ups and the downs. It's a movement of ego-aside improvement from all angles. We are the next generation of bosses, and the coolest thing is we don't have to wait until we are fifty-five to step into that role. We can do it now!

Many of you already own and operate your own businesses, and that's why you're here. First, congratulations! You are in the 16 percent of people who choose to create their own destinies, of people who refuse to work all day building someone else's dream—you're an entrepreneur. I hope this book can reaffirm some messages that you already practice in your daily work. I hope it can be a beacon of hope for you during down times and remind you that the work you're doing is important. I hope you read something that gives you joy or peace or comfort or sparks a new idea for you on a difficult day. I am excited you're here and welcome to the YoungBoss family!

According to the Oxford Languages dictionary, an entrepreneur is defined as "a person who organizes and operates a business or businesses, taking on greater than normal financial risks to do so." Well damn!

Just hit us where it hurts. Capital is almost always an issue, amongst other things like staffing, stamina, and marketing. So let's cover it all! But I also want to remind you, "Although business owners come in all ages, according to **NBCS**, 35 percent of entrepreneurs and small business owners are in the 50-59 age bracket, followed by 40-49-year-olds. In fact, about 60 percent of people who start small businesses are between the ages of 40-60."[1] Zippia.com says that only 6 percent of small business owners are between the ages of 20-30.[2] We are the minority here! Being a young business owner is a huge feat! You had an idea, saw the challenges ahead, and you said, "It's worth it. I'll do whatever it takes." You know that if it's important to you, you'll find a way, and if not, you'll find an excuse. This IS important to you. Bringing your idea to life is magic!

I can't wait to see where this journey takes you, and I'm excited to be a part of it. I truly wish you all the success in the world. You're smart, you're motivated, you're on the verge of doing something big! Let's go at it together, young boss!

---

1 "20 Entrepreneur Statistics You Need to Know (2023)," Apollo Technical, Jan. 12, 2023, https://www.apollotechnical.com/entrepreneur-statistics/.

2 Zippia, "40 Stand-Out Small Business Statistics [2023]: How Many Small Businesses Are In The United States?" Zippia.com, Feb. 9, 2023, https://www.zippia.com/advice/small-business-statistics/.

Chapter 2
WHAT GOT ME HERE

Where to begin… my journey to leadership started as many stories begin, at the bottom. When I first started working for my father, I was his assistant. No formal training, just sitting beside him and anticipating his needs. I learned what made his life easier, did those things, and then sought ways to improve. I had no background or experience. It was on-the-job training.

My role quickly went from organizing his office to booking his travel arrangements until, one day, he asked me to come to work events with him, and I became a "booth babe." He would say the spiel when people would come to the booth, and I'd listen two to three times and then parrot what he said. He was never the type to say, "Good job!" enthusiastically, like I am. Instead, he was the type to say, "That was good, but next time, say…"

You've got to be okay with being an A-minus student. That's how I learned. I asked questions, but never too many. More importantly, I wrote everything down, and I listened. Learning through osmosis is hard for some. I understand it's not how everyone works. But to be honest, my father never once taught me how to speak from the stage, and yet the first time I took the stage to sell, I sold over $1 million. Osmosis works!

Memories are tied to emotions. I watched my father on stage for twenty-plus years of my life, and I felt emotional when he was up there, whether it was good or bad. It was what it was. My memories of him teaching and training are tied to emotions. So when it came time for me to practice, it just naturally came out of me. Something I had zero desire to do, something that people are terrified of doing, just flew out of me with incredible ease. My dad honed his skills of being an entrepreneur, business owner, and professional speaker.

I had so many beautiful memories of him over the years that I never knew I needed until the time came. For example, one time on a work trip, he made ZERO sales, or an "egg" as we call it. We were in Philadelphia at a Hilton Garden Inn. We had paid for some radio promotions to fill the room for us. I was working the event, making sure it was smooth, sorting out all the details. He gave his pitch, just like he'd done a million times before, and after four hours of presenting, he went for the close, smooth as ever. He truly was a rockstar salesman. I was waiting in the back of the room excitedly, as I knew this was the part of the day when I'd get bombarded with people trying to buy the products and services. Every person gave me a smile or wave and proceeded to leave one by one. I was SHOOK! I'd never seen it happen. My dad was an amazing salesman, and this was the first time I saw him fail. When the room was finally empty, he looked at me and I at him. I felt terrible. He didn't do anything wrong. Maybe the crowd was broke. I thought, *Screw them! They're not right for us anyway!*

As I gathered all the leftover flyers and pens and cleaned the room up, I could sense my father was a little disappointed, but he finally said to me, "Pack up and get dressed. We are going to dinner." I did exactly that, and as we sat at dinner, I thought about all the time he spent preparing for his presentations. I thought about the work he put in; he just gave his heart and soul for FOUR HOURS, not to mention the cost of renting the meeting space at the hotel, providing food for those who came, bringing all the materials, our two hotel rooms, our flights, our rental car, the radio ads, etc. As I was adding up the costs,

I realized a lesson about being a business owner. You cannot control the outcome. You do your best every day, and the repetition pays off in the end, but you cannot control the outcome.

My dad finally turned to me, once we had our wine, and said, "Ya know, I've gotten many eggs before, but this may be my first one in over fifteen years." He laughed his joyful belly laugh, toasted me, and we ordered our meal. Right then and there, I learned the most important lesson of all: ***you have to let things go.*** He did not let this egg stop his progress. He did not even really let it control the rest of his day. He laughed it off! Because guess what? It happens! It happens to everyone, even the best of the best. If you've never failed, success isn't all that sweet. Failure is necessary. My respect for my father/my boss in that moment grew tenfold. His maturity was immense, and it taught me a lesson I never knew I would need. Laugh it off! It happens!

We then sat for the next twenty minutes and discussed what could have gone better and where we made mistakes. I cannot thank my father enough for his "Don't let them get you down" attitude. We deemed him Mr. Positive when I was a child because, even in the face of disappointment, he never failed to be his true self. He was positive to a fault. He never spoke poorly of the people in the room; he never said anything negative about them. He told me that God was protecting us from the wrong buyers.

Eight years later, when I was in San Diego, I pitched the best I could and at the end of the night earned a whopping ZERO sales. So I went to the hotel lobby, grabbed a bottle of wine, toasted myself, laughed, thought of Dad, and got up the next day to do it again. One egg down, many more to come! Such is life! The best thing about it was that I was flooded with memories of my dad. If I had never worked with him, if I had never taken that trip and been his right-hand girl, I wouldn't have had that moment or memory. Memories are tied to emotions. Losing my father in 2021, I underestimated how many moments just like this one would eventually return to the forefront of my mind and remind me of how much I learned being by his side. As people say, "Kids don't listen to what you say. They watch what you do." Well, I was his kid, but I wasn't a kid, yet I watched everything he did. I soaked it all up. I caught when he taught, and for that, I am the luckiest girl in the world.

Throughout the years working by my father's side, I did something that, in hindsight, I think was vital to my success. I worked every position in our company. I never planned it this way. It just happened. First, I started as his assistant, then did all the finances for him and our companies. Shortly thereafter, I became the event planner running all events in and out of state and even a National Convention—mind you, this is all with ZERO experience, just learning on the fly. I eventually became our social media coordinator and marketing manager, working with ad agencies, copywriters, and website editors. I got a second cell phone I carried with me everywhere and became a phone sales team member as well, picking up every call that came in from 4:00 a.m.—11:00 p.m. I was addicted to that phone! I did the HR, hiring and firing people as needed. I did the customer service, dealing with any and all angry and happy customers via phone, email, or in person. I was a travel concierge, tax prep consultant, transaction specialist, CRM manager, you name it, I did it. EXCEPT speaking on stage! That was the one position I vehemently declined.

I eventually settled into my favorite position, which was Operations Director. I really enjoyed planning and running the events, dealing with all the customers and processing sales, etc. It quickly became second nature to me. Except I was also still doing all the other positions mentioned above. I've said it once. And I'll say it twice. One of my superpowers is my capacity. Most people have a plate that they fill up with work, health, family, pets, etc. I have a platter. I don't know how or why, but God blessed me with a supernatural gift to have A LOT on my plate and not feel overwhelmed or stressed. I love it, actually. It drives me. Every day, I look at what needs to be done and prioritize from most to least important and will guarantee to get at least a minimum of 95 percent of all the things done. When others look at the list, they may think it's a list of a week's worth of things, but for me, it's a challenge, and it lights me up! Pumping out quality work, staying on top of things, and being my best self are my favorite things to bring to the work world.

After a few years working in this high-capacity role, our business consultant suggested my dad hire an Integrator or a Chief Operations Officer and then delegate and elevate some of the staff. The business consultant was thinking about me, but wasn't sure Dad caught it at first. Then, a few hours later, in the same meeting, when we were running numbers, he looked my dad dead in the eyes and said, "I hope you're paying her well because she is the backbone of this company. She could be stolen from you in a heartbeat and paid handsomely. Don't tempt her." It was in that moment that my dad looked at me and realized, *Oh man… you are not just my 'little' assistant anymore. You've helped me grow this business from two people to fifteen. You've done every position possible. You've hired and fired. You've made us ten times our profits because I no longer have to focus on them. Holy cow, you're a rockstar.*

I just want to state there is nothing wrong with asking for a raise or asking to move up in your prospective role or company. It's just not my typical MO. I have always thought that instead of asking, you let your work shine. My father came to me a few weeks later and said, "I am looking to hire someone for COO. I was considering your uncle, unless you have any other ideas…?" At first, I was offended, thinking, *How could you choose him over me, when I do it ALL? He does only one role, sales. Come on!* But I also logically understood his brother was older and had more experience. And maybe he deserved it.

So I told him, "If that's what you want, I get it. I'll help train him. You just let me know what you want the contract to reflect and I'll get it back to you ASAP." I turned away, disappointed. Later that evening,

I was chatting with my mother about the interaction, and I said, "I don't know why he wouldn't consider me."

She faced me directly and said, "Do you want the position?" I assured her I did, and she reminded me, "Ask and you might just receive."

I went back to my father the following day and asked him if we could speak about the open role. I showed him all I had built and had been working on over the last few years. I told him I wanted to put my name in the hat for the open position. He smiled so big and said, "I thought you would never ask."

My internal reaction was like, *WAIT, WHAT!!!???* But on the outside, I tried my best to stay calm and just asked him, "What do you mean?"

He said, "I would never want to put pressure on you or any of my kids. I love that you enjoy working with me, but the last thing I want is to put you into something that you don't want to be in. I want you to work with me as long as you do, and the day you don't, I will be 100 percent okay with that and help you on your way to find something new and different. You do not need or have to feel tied to this or to me." I understood at that moment that my father was just looking out for his children. He had been a solopreneur his whole life. He never had a large team. He never had children who wanted to work for him. He was in new territory, and he was hesitant about tying me down to something he wasn't sure I loved. I reassured him that this was the best job I ever had. Work-life balance was great, and I got a thrill out of how everything was new every day. I loved learning all the roles and growing the business, and, most importantly, I adored working by his side. I was working with him because I wanted to be there and for no other reason. It wasn't the money. I knew I could have been paid more elsewhere. Nor was it the role. I knew I could be putting in way less work somewhere else. No, I absolutely relished being by his side in a work environment, and I never wanted that experience to stop.

I am blessed that I found a role that gave me an opportunity to realize my God-given skills. Not everyone has that opportunity in life, and I am beyond grateful I got to try over ten different roles within one company to determine where my skills lie. My father gave me the role of COO, and our relationship bloomed even more. It sounds funny to say, but I truly was his "work wife." We spent every day together whether in person, on the phone, or Zoom. I was always there for him, anticipating every need. Over the following years, we grew from fifteen team members to over fifty. He brought new ideas to the table almost daily, and we learned how to work together as a Visionary and Integrator should. (I'll explain those two roles in Chapter 32 in depth.) Although I always tested higher than him as a Visionary, I let him take that lead. He would bring up new ideas and businesses, as a Visionary does, and I would listen intently. From there, I'd write it all down, and as the Integrator, I'd flesh it out, coming up with the timeframes, who would need to be involved, the steps to make it happen, and the cost that it would take to bring the idea to fruition. At our next meeting, I would present how it would look, and he would poke holes and say yes or no. He wasn't a details guy, but he was phenomenal when it came to the big picture. He was most definitely a dreamer. I love the fact that our working style allowed him to be a dreamer. He could run wild with his ideas because he knew he had someone tying him back down to earth. An Integrator's job is never to tell their boss NO; it's to tell them HOW. I think that's vital to remember.

One of the biggest lessons I learned when it came to becoming the COO is that all eyes are on you. I was the youngest person in the company, and while my father never treated me like I was young, some of the other staff couldn't help but do so. It made me work harder to present myself as professional and mature. And I think that ended up being a real benefit for me. You see, most of the people in the real estate training space are middle-aged gentlemen, and they've all known each other for years—an old boys' club, you could say. Our typical client was a fifty- to sixty-year-old man who had been in different forms of real estate his whole life. I had little to nothing in common with these clients and business partners, but I learned what they liked and didn't like and what they wanted to talk about. I became who I needed to become to thrive in this specific world.

Sometimes you have to look around and say, "What got me here won't get me there." Like that person who was perfect for the five-man team may not be right for a 100-person corporate company. You have to look around and check your systems, staffing, and processes to see if they've kept up with the needs of the business. It's been vital to become the person I need to be to get the things I'm looking for.

Chapter 3
DOIN' IT AND DOIN' IT AND DOIN' IT WELL

One of the greatest blessings in my career has been working every position within our company. This isn't always possible, but when you're an entrepreneur, it's likely you'll have to do so. I once heard that if you want to buy a Dutch Bros franchise, you must work for two years, or more, as a barista to know what they go through and get the true experience of what it's like to be an employee for the company. It gives you great appreciation. We all understand this concept, but I think it's very true. In our businesses, whenever it was time to delegate and elevate, I would write down everything I was doing for the role, map out all the processes and procedures, and then look to hire. Whenever we hired someone new, I would train with them and work side by side with them until they understood the role and could do it on their own.

In hiring, one of the most crucial lessons I learned was to LISTEN. You see, I could have come in with a big ego thinking I knew best, but I would have missed valuable opportunities. One of my first hires was actually my now sister-in-law, but then she was my brother's girlfriend. She and I got along swimmingly, but when it came to work, we had different approaches. I would teach her what to do, and she would come back to me and say, "Well, have you thought about doing it this way?"

At first, my reaction was "NOPE! Do it my way!"

But when I attempted to understand her and explained my side of the story, she would say, "Okay, I see why now. I'll do it that way."

At other times I would say, "Why don't you try it your way and let's review at the end if it was truly better?" She was a rockstar at the 'lazy girl method!' And if you can't tell already, that's the exact opposite of my work personality. She found so many shortcuts to automate things to make them less manual and more seamless. I am grateful for her attitude and ability to ask for what she needed to get her job done in a more succinct way. If I was an asshole boss who she couldn't talk to and who wasn't willing to hear her out, she would have either A) done those things behind my back, pissed me off, and gotten fired, or B) been miserable thinking every day that she could be doing this easier, better, and faster if someone would just listen to her!

I'm very grateful for our friendship and working relationships, and I treat all of my staff the exact same way, no matter their role. I'll tell them how I've done it and empower them to tell me if they see an easier method. Reality is **your way is not always the best way.** Sometimes you need someone to come in and ask WHY! The key is to be open to their feedback and not take it personally. It's not about you! You hired them for a reason, and to be honest, the best thing you could ever do is hire someone to do something better, faster, and cheaper than you could! If I hire someone and I still have to do half the work, or they have NO ideas on how to make the role better, it's actually not the right person for ME. Maybe in your business you want cogs, people who sit there and do the job and don't ask questions, but for me, that tends to be correlated with a lack of innovation and creativity. And I just can't jive with it. Now, I'm not asking everyone to come up with grandiose ideas for the company. But I am requiring all staff to dig deep into their role and make it their own and, most importantly, do better than I ever did in that same position. Their goal is to beat me. I found $50K we could spend elsewhere or save. How much can you find? I sold thirty out of fifty calls. How many are you closing? I ran fifteen-plus events in one year all by myself. How many can you do? I traveled practically every weekend to work booths and promoted the company. Are you willing to do the same or more? Having boundaries is good, nothing wrong with that, but the attitude of acting your wage is bullshit. Unfortunately, this attitude is spreading in the work culture and environment, and it's in direct opposition to an entrepreneurial mindset. It may work for a nine-to-five basic corporate job, but don't ever come looking for a job from me or another entrepreneur with that attitude. It's the exact opposite energy of what we're trying to achieve. We ***do what it takes to get the job done, no matter what.***

Chapter 4
CAN YOU HANDLE THE COMMISSION?

A really hard lesson for me was how much more Sales makes than every other position. I learned this early on. And it's specifically tough when you feel you are doing EVERYTHING! I remember when my father asked me to gather all the information for taxes. When I saw what the salesman, who flew in for eight events annually, made, I almost cried! How could this be?! I worked day in and day out, slaving away at my job. Don't get me wrong. I enjoyed it. But what? How? It wasn't a little off from my pay rate; the difference was drastic. I learned some valuable lessons in that moment. First, if you're asking someone to look at your books, make sure they feel fairly compensated. You don't want that to be the breaking moment of your working relationship. Second, when I approached my father about this unfair pay structure, he calmly and easily explained to me they are paid in full commission and do not get a salary or flat rate. He then asked me, "Do you want to do sales and only eat what you kill? I'll teach you." I thought about it for a second. Well, wait. That meant if I sucked or the people weren't buying and I didn't sell, I made nothing!? UMMMM, no thanks, Dad! I stuck with my salary for the following few years, but it was a tough lesson.

Since I learned this lesson with my father, some interesting things have happened. I have changed my thought process entirely.

Commission structures are thrilling, and I understand the draw to them, but they don't work for everyone. You see, we all have six human needs we have to meet, and some prioritize one more than others, but one of those needs is certainty. Another one of those needs is uncertainty. Someone who places certainty in the top one or two of their six needs probably won't be taking a commission pay structure anytime soon. My sister is someone who would fall into this category. But someone who loves and craves uncertainty would excel in a commission-only role. **You have to know your strengths and play to them.** This doesn't mean you can't grow and change, but it does mean you are who you are naturally, and unless you're actively trying to change that, you're not going to… let's be real!

Sales can be a scary role, a role that is not consistent or steady, but for those who are confident in their skills, it can be a very rewarding career. I highly encourage everyone, especially a young person, to try a commission-only sales role at some point in their life. You will hone your skills and learn a lot about yourself and other people. You see, all of life is sales, and you cannot avoid it. You can pretend you hate it, or don't want anything to do with it, but at the end of the day, you're selling yourself at every moment, every hour, and if you don't learn to love this, you will fail when it comes to getting things you want.

Personally, when I learned what the sales team was making compared to me, I was pissed. Then when I learned the risk they were taking, I backed off, but I kept a close eye on them and practiced my own sales skills until I felt confident enough to do it too. I took over our company phone line and made it a point to practice my skills with every person calling in, identifying their needs and their pains and then working to bring them to a solution. At first, I sucked. I would get stuck on the phone answering questions for forty-five minutes, and then they wouldn't even buy… terrible! And then I changed, I learned and leaned into mentors who rocked, and I started to improve. Sales became exciting to me. Each call became a challenge that was for me and only me. Eventually, they took me off the phones, and we built an entire phone sales team, but for the five years prior, it was me, honing my interpersonal skills, practicing with each inquiring caller. It was the best practice I could ever have been given; my only wish is that I got it sooner.

Now I am honored to hold the main-stage presenter role at our company, where I get the opportunity to enroll incredible investors and entrepreneurs into our program eight times per year. At these events, I am blessed that we have an amazing product to sell and people really understand and come alongside the mission of the company. Although our closing percentages are far beyond industry standard, every time I'm in a room of experienced salespeople, I still soak up all the advice I can get. I will never stop learning. It doesn't matter if I closed every person in the room—there is still somewhere I could grow and learn!

Chapter 5
DO YOU TRUST ME?

One thing that I think has always worked to my advantage is being a trustworthy confidant for my team members. I focused on building trust in relation to seven different categories: competence, character, confidence, caring, communication, consistency, and commitment. I believe every team needs someone they know they can go to when they need to share intimate details of their struggles at work. Or someone to whom they can ask questions and know they're not going to be shut down. Many of my team members know I am the go-to gal for any of their needs, and they're not afraid to ask me for help. I think that's a beautiful thing. Aiming to be trustworthy all across the board in those seven categories will change the way you interact with your team. You want to be trusted across the board. It helps me keep my pulse on the company and what everyone is struggling with; it also helps me grow closer to them.

When we hire someone new, we have them take a Predictive Index quiz which gives us insight on their God-given skills. For me, this part is important. It's not about determining how smart they are; it's about how fast the sponge can soak up water. When someone tests below a 250 on this cognitive scoring system, I know they may need me to tell them things four to five times before they understand them fully. If it's a high score in the 300-400s, then I know they are the type I tell something to once, maybe twice, and they've got it! This is incredibly helpful when training someone new on your team because the frustration levels can increase significantly, especially if you're more of an impatient person, like I am, and someone asks you a million times how to do something. But once I know what they need, I can accommodate. My team can trust me because they know I won't blow up on them or be upset if they need to ask me for clarification or how to do something again. I will always retrain them to use the tools I gave them in the first place, in a way that gives them peace and understanding. They know I care and genuinely want them to learn and grow. It fosters a culture of hard work and dedication.

There's another way I show my team I care. I personally like to learn everything I can about them. I want to know their love languages—in the workplace they're called the "five appreciations in the workplace." I want to know their pets' names, partners' names, what other businesses they're involved with, what they do for fun on the weekends, how they spend their holidays, and their favorite place to eat. For me, investing in my team pays back tenfold. So I truly want to know these things, learn them, and use them in our daily interactions and conversations to relate with more depth.

Finally, trust is something that is shaped by how I prioritize the company. If there's one thing that's important to portray as a young boss, it's putting the company first, before yourself or anyone else. Your team needs to know where your priorities lie. If they know you will choose the company over yourself, they will trust you. If they know you will choose the company over them, they will respect you. It's a balance. It's not personal. There's a lot of things in life and business that I think are 100 percent personal, but when it comes down to choices, you cannot allow this to slip. Choosing the company first keeps your integrity high and everyone on a level playing field. If someone is not hitting Key Performance Indicators or KPIs continuously, but they have a wonderful personality, and you love seeing their face at work every day… sorry, it's not best for the company. They need to find another role in the business, or they need to go. If you are doing more than you should be doing and aren't the right person for the job, you need to stop doing it and delegate to someone else. You're wasting the company's time and money by doing it yourself!

By choosing the company first, you are actually showing a lot of integrity and not favoritism. It's an honorable thing to do, as long as you're being honest with yourself. This concept goes hand in hand with predictability. I think it's important to be predictable in your decision-making as a boss. When you are all over the place, and sometimes let things slide, and other times are a hardass, it's going to create a culture of unsettled fear. The team needs to see and know that you make the same choices and decisions, whether they are in the room or not. Doing so breeds an immense amount of respect and trust. If you are predictable, they can make choices they know will please you. If you are constantly switching it up on them, they will never know what you actually want or need. It's that simple. Say you have a situation where you have a team of phone sales members. When one of them doesn't hit their $30,000/month goal for two months in a row, they go on "warning" for fifteen more days. And if they aren't at $15,000 in the following fifteen days, they're fired. You've held to this for the last seven months, but now all of a sudden, you let Peter stay because you're short on phone sales people and you need the body. He was on warning, but you kept him even though he didn't hit the $15,000. Now it's day twenty-one because you'd rather have someone than not have someone. No! You have to stay consistent. It is not best for the business. Let him go, find someone else, and step up in the meantime to help out or ask the team to step up. They would rather work overtime than watch you work out of fear because this then gives them mixed messages about what is or isn't the integrity level of this company. A person's values should be congruent with and evident in their actions. **Choose the company first. Be predictable with your actions.**

Chapter 6
CAPRICORN ENERGY...

Let's talk about the "hardest worker in the room mentality" for a moment. This one is difficult for me because I genuinely flourish within a hardworking company, but I want to give you a huge warning. I unknowingly built a culture of no work-life-balance, and I "broke" some of my employees. It wasn't a good situation, and I want you to avoid it.

You see, I have a very high capacity for work and being able to squeeze in what I need personally. Also, side note, you should know, I REALLY LOVE TO WORK! Capricorn much?! For example, I love to merge my regular life with my work life in ways like the following. Being outside is self-care and totally therapeutic for me, so I will spend one to two hours outside while working each day. I'm able to spend time and play with my dog, get my outdoor nature self-care time, and pump out work. This is totally fun for me and absolutely gets me energized for the rest of the day. Or taking calls in the car. I don't need to listen to music 24-7, so while driving, I maximize my time and take meetings or calls in the car. On vacations, I am an early riser. When everyone else is sleeping in, I get up early and pump out one to three hours of work, maybe even a meeting or two.

Now for me, all of this works. I get to be on vacation, spend time outside, and drive to my facial or massage appointment while getting work done at the same time. I excel in multitasking. But while I was doing this and thinking it was the best thing for myself and my business, I noticed my staff was doing the same. Joe took a vacation to Legoland with his kids and answered my calls and emails…. Ummm, NO! He was supposed to be with his kids. Why would he answer me!? STOP! But here's the thing—why wouldn't he? First, I, his boss was emailing him while he was supposed to be out enjoying family time, and second, I answered all his emails while I was out on vacation. I took meetings and calls and didn't stop. I had unknowingly built a tradition of work with no time for play. I genuinely wanted Joe to enjoy this vacation and have time with his kids, so I replied by encouraging him to drop all work and spend time with his family. Then I noticed it happened again with another employee. She was supposed to be with her sister who was sick in the hospital, and yes, she was physically there, but she was taking a meeting with me in the hospital! What the hell!? "Cancel this meeting. Stop working. Why do you even have your laptop there?! Take the time off! Come on!" I told her all of those things, but no matter how much I encouraged and told my team to take time off, I noticed it wasn't changing anything.

It's similar to having kids. TELLING them to do something may or MAY NOT work. In this case, it surely wasn't working. My team needed proof they were allowed to take time off. This all came to a head when one of my team members shared that his wife wanted to leave him because he was traveling so much. I told you already. I seriously love to work, but not everyone's the same. And it's not that my team members don't "love to work." It's not that at all. It's that I've built my life around my company and my job. It's my pride and joy, and I get everything else I need in. I work out in the mornings and spend time with my family and pets. I get my house clean and organized. I get to shop and relax with spa days. I get to travel with friends. I truly have time for it all. AND I can pump out an immense amount of work. Here's the thing. I am an anomaly, and if you're reading this and you're a young boss like me, you may be feeling the same thing. The amount of work you can produce is tenfold what others seemingly can. You may feel like you have it all. Why can't they balance their lives the same way? Reality check, you are special, and they are not bad or wrong because they can't. I realized that asking my staff to not work to my standards of work wasn't going to happen. They needed me to set the tone. Just because I can be a workhorse doesn't mean I should be. They needed me to take a true break. Not a break where I was multitasking, a real respite. A vacation where I didn't answer my phone and left my emails unopened. They needed to see me do it.

The challenge was set. I picked a trip and marked on my calendar that I was out of the office. Actually, I wrote BELLE BLOCKED, and guess what? They called, they emailed, they texted because I had trained them to do so. What they didn't expect was I was truly living up to what I had told them I'd do. I trusted that if they REALLY needed something dire, I would somehow find out about it, and that they could handle 99.9 percent of the situations without me. I hired them for many reasons, and this was one. So I shut off my email, and phone, and lived in the moment. My head and feet were in the same place... FOR ONCE in my life! And I'll tell ya, although I love to work and multitask, it felt... good! The team slowly started calling less, and I stayed strong and didn't answer. When I got back in town and we had our first meeting, they updated me on their wins, losses, and struggles. While doing so, they beamed with pride. I knew I did something right, but it wasn't a one-time thing. I had to do it again. I had to cement in them that I wanted and needed them to behave this way, that I meant it when I asked them to have work-life balance.

I went to a vision retreat, and they taught me to build my schedule with my personal goals first, blocking out the time for workouts, time with friends and family, time with God, or any other personal things like playing golf or basketball or hiking, etc. THEN they had me fill in the calendar with work. I did it and encouraged my staff to do it too. I started noticing small events pop up on their calendars, like Joe's. He added all his kids' after-school activities, so I could see gymnastics and soccer practice. And Melisa added her noon workouts with her trainer. Jason added walks with the dogs and morning coffee with his wife. All this made me so happy. So my next trip I did the same thing. I wrote BELLE BLOCKED and let them all know during the weekly meeting that I would be out from Wednesday to the following Monday. I told them that if they felt the temptation to reach out, they should ask themselves if it could wait until Monday and, if it couldn't, that they mobilize to make the best decision on their own. I told them I trusted them and thanked them for respecting my time.

This time, the calls were cut by a fourth! They were catching on! I meant business. They could call, but I wasn't going to answer. I wanted them to do the same when it came time for them to step away from work. Jason had a vacation the following month, and he really grasped it. He didn't respond to us, he wasn't at the meetings, and he waited until arriving back into the office to dive into any of the issues at hand. It was working! It wasn't the words. It wasn't the request to block their time off. It was my doing it and sticking to it. I had to **show them what work-life balance looks like, not by faking it, but by truly doing it.** The hustler has to die for the CEO to live! Now when any one of us goes on vacation, the entire team respects the trips so much that we don't send that person anything while they are gone. No texts, calls, or emails except texts to say, "I hope you have an amazing trip" or "Travel safely; tell the kids we say hi!" etc.

This shift in our company changed everything. It had to start at the top. It was vital. They weren't going to take on what I was saying if I also wasn't going to abide by the same rules. No one wants their boss to outwork them, and that's how they were feeling. Now I get to take true vacations and enjoy myself, and they get to have real time off, spent with people they love. So, listen, the moral of the story is don't worry about being the hardest worker in the room. If you're the boss, odds are you already are that person. You may have to evaluate to see what kind of environment you are breeding in the opposite direction. Actions speak louder than words, and you may not know the impact you're having. Your staff want to impress you, but your job is to protect them. Ruining marriages, having kids grow up with parents who are always working, having your staff be out of shape because they don't have any time to work out, these are all things that don't breed a healthy work life. We want to encourage them to work hard and play hard, to live life in a way that suits their goals.

Chapter 7
THE FUTURE IS BRIGHT. CAN YOU SEE IT?

As I mentioned in the last chapter, I highly encourage young bosses and their teams to vision-set their lives and build their business around it. Not the opposite way around. That looks like creating a blank calendar and crafting your perfect week. When do you want to work out and for how long? How does it make you feel? When do you want to see friends or family? Your kids or partner? What fun hobbies or activities do you want to incorporate in your weekly life? How often? Is church or therapy or self-care something that is a priority to you? How often do you want to participate in those activities, and what does it look or feel like when you do? Once you've mapped out your dream week, look at it and see where work fits in! I know, crazy! You might think you can't build your personal life first and your work life second, but guess what? You work for yourself, and you absolutely can. No one and nothing is stopping you but yourself.

This method of vision setting has changed my life and the lives of many other young bosses because it starts with building a life that you actually want to live. And, reality check, there is a lot less time for work in your schedule, which forces you to be more productive with the time you have. You only get one life, and you don't want to wither away at a desk or behind a computer screen. You want to live the life you've dreamed. On the YoungBoss Podcast, we often refer to vision setting and ask our guests if their business matches the vision they've set for their life. Many times they get caught up in the day-to-day hustle, and they'll look down and tell me, unfortunately, no, it's not on track with what they want. And it's okay—we all get sidetracked—but it's also something you have to be actively pursuing. You need to share it with those who are close to you, meaning your Integrator, COO, or right-hand man or woman, as well as your life partner, if you have one.

It's not enough to create the vision and let it sit there. You must actively read it. You must attach emotions and feelings to it. When your Integrator knows the vision for your life and, in turn, the business, they can help you. My staff will often ask me, "And does that fit the vision?" It's just that slight reminder it isn't the right thing for me to be spending my time doing. My guess is you didn't create a company to be a slave to it. You created something because you wanted freedom. Whatever the reason, living a life that fits your vision is how you stay in the freedom zone. It's the only way! I highly advise if you haven't done this exercise, or one like it, to try it today. Get it all out. What does this dream life feel like? Look like? Sound like? Who gets the most from you in terms of attention? Time? Admiration? What does your financial stability look like? How does that make you feel? How often do you check on it? What does your work/company/business do for you? How does it aid you in making your dream life real?

Also, keep in mind, if you can't vision set for your own personal life, how are you going to do that for your business? As a Visionary, your job is to "know when to hold 'em and know when to fold 'em" as Kevin Harrington from *Shark Tank* says! You are literally tasked with knowing the future, seeing the future, and predicting what moves your company into the future. These skills are vital to maintaining longevity in business and securing your place in the market. Here today, gone tomorrow, is what happens to people with no direction or vision. They get lost when the wind blows! You must realize your personal vision and your business vision to succeed!

Chapter 8
HABITUAL HABITS

One of the most common traits of successful young bosses is a commitment to forging strong habits. IYKYK! When it comes to building a business, a brand, a legacy, it helps to have consistency and habits that aid you in your journey to the top. I'm not just talking about #thatgirl habits, but they give us a great place to start! Waking up early, making your bed, and getting healthy liquids in your body before hitting your workout are all great ways to start your day in a positive way. So are reading books that are good for the soul and good for growth, spending time outside in nature, being around your partner or kids, and prioritizing self-care. You might also go to therapy or church or a place where you can mentally express the things you hold in. These are all habits that every young boss should be cultivating, not just for themselves and their best practices, but also to lead and leave an example to their staff. How is my staff going to believe me that I care about their health and fitness journey when I don't care about mine? It has to come from an authentic, genuine place. And guess what? If you don't care about it, that's fine. It's just part of the culture you'll be building! I personally like to be mindful of it. I don't necessarily care that my staff is comprised of the fittest, healthiest people on the planet, but I do care that they have the time and capacity to be. It's my job as a boss to respect their life choices and to give them the opportunity to balance their work and their life, not overwhelm them.

I personally like to start my day by ending my day in a good place. I mean that before bed, I like to clean the kitchen and living spaces, so it's all set up for a nice work day the following day. If you don't do this, try it! I swear it'll help you be more clear-headed in the morning. I make sure my office is spick and span before I leave, and if I watch TV or read a book before bed, I clean up the space I enjoyed that activity in before going to bed. So when I wake up, the house, the office, the kitchen, the bathroom—you name it—is ready to go for me! I feel fresh and ready because my environment is prepped. I start the day by continuing that habitual method of making the bed and leaving the bedroom how I want to find it… perfect! I know it sounds psychotic, and if you're a messy one, I get it. This is asking a lot! But I promise those small habits really enable you to be more focused on larger issues throughout the day.

Other habits that really help me succeed as a young boss are finishing what I started and keeping distractions to a minimum. For me, that looks like putting my phone on focus mode and blocking enough time to not just start but fully complete the projects at hand. If I don't have enough time to complete it, I won't start it. I'll choose a smaller project and block more time for it later. This really helps me keep my list of priorities in order and block my time to focus on the things that really matter, hence getting more things accomplished in one day.

Some good advice for creating and sustaining good habits… just start! **Start where you are. Use what you have. Begin today!** The hardest part is starting, but the more you practice your new habits, the better and easier they will become! I really believe that when you set new goals in business, in life, wherever, it all comes down to the small things you can begin doing right away. For example, if you want to start writing a book, block the time off first in your calendar. Second, find yourself a quiet space that instills creativity in you. Third, no excuses.

When that time comes and you're supposed to be writing, sit down and do it! Maybe your goal is 2,000 words every time you sit down, but you can only get 500. That's okay. Do something every day that your future self will thank you for! It's clearly going to take you longer than you think, but those small habits of blocking the time, having the space, and just typing away will eventually turn you into a writer and help you complete that big goal of yours.

Here's another tip. When you connect existing habits to one another, they can strengthen your resolve. If you want to write a book, then tie it to something you already do. Maybe you take a bath every day, and now you're going to leave a notepad and pen by the bath. That way, when you go into the tub, it's there for you to link to the habit you already have. Jot down some thoughts. Let your creativity flow. Setting yourself up for success is always the way to go about creating motivation. It's important because you're going to hit roadblocks, and you would be remiss if you didn't preemptively prepare for them.

Habits are baby steps, but they can help you create the life you dream of if you hold onto them. One small step at a time, step by step. Whatever they may be, those habits will eventually turn into major lifestyle changes, and you'll be more than pleased with the results. Like they say, "How do you eat an elephant? One bite at a time!" Step by step, it's the stairs, not the staircase, that matters. We are all on our own journeys, and comparing yourself to others will never help you reach your best potential.

Chapter 9
KNOW THYSELF

When it comes to starting a business, one of the most beneficial and important things you can do for yourself is learn who you are and how you tick. In short, know thyself! **Being a leader will bring out many different sides of you, and it will push you to new limits you never knew existed,** so the more you know about yourself and how and why you operate in certain ways, the easier it can be to anticipate, understand, and move forward. If you don't know how you come off, you can be misinterpreted by other team members, investors, or customers.

Knowing how you present and how others internalize it matters. Being a friend or family member and coming off one way isn't the same as being someone's boss. Everything you do is amplified, and they're going to take more offense at your comments, behavior, and lack of attention. If you aren't in the mood when you're at a family gathering, your family may not think anything of it. Maybe they ask you what's wrong, and you respond you don't feel well or had a rough week, and they all accept it and move on. If you're in a bad mood at a weekly team meeting, your team members or employees may be nervous to ask you what's up and instead internalize that you are mad at them. They may interpret your mood to mean they are doing poor work and, sometimes, at the most extreme, conclude you are going to fire them. This is something to be mindful of because if you're unaware of how your behavior is being interpreted, it can lead to an insecure work environment for your team. Now I'm not saying you have to be happy 24-7, but it's about sharing what's going on if you're not happy. You might therefore start a meeting by saying, "Hey, guys, I'm not in the best mood today. It has nothing to do with any of you or your performances. I am just not feeling great. I want everyone to know that I value you here, and my facial expression or attitude is just off right now. I will get over it, and I will bring my best self to work today because I would want you to do the same for me. So please note, I'm good, and I am thankful for each of you. Let's start this meeting and have a great day!" And then seriously do your best to be your best self that day. Turn that frown upside down! Even if you don't, your team knows what's going on and that it's not a *them* thing—it's a *you* thing. This will ease a lot of unrest.

On the YoungBoss Podcast, we also talk about how it's vital to not just know how you come off personally, but how you present your skill set as well. As an entrepreneur, many people wear all the hats in the beginning. But as you grow, and have more team members, it's important to know your highest and best use as a leader. What are your natural God-given skills, and how can you dive into those to live in your superpower? If you don't know, I highly suggest using the quadrant method (I'll share more about in a later chapter) and determine what you do really like about your role so you can sit in that power and delegate and elevate! My friend Kyle has a terrible time with this, and I'm always reminding him to work ON his business, not IN it. Anytime a new contract is acquired with his company, his first inclination is to take it on himself. He'll convince himself, and try to convince me, that this is the best thing. He can save money! He has the time! He can swing by after doing the first three contracts and checking on his seven teams and running meetings and, and... AND I remind him it's not his highest and best use. He could hire someone else to do this job, and YES, he would make less money, but he would be giving them an opportunity to make some money, and he wouldn't have to do it himself. PLUS, if he continues to do the contracts himself, he's not going to be able to scale. He will eventually run out of time, capacity, and energy! Instead, he could spend his time more wisely by outsourcing and finding staff to work this new contract so he can onboard ten new contracts, and in turn, make a WHOLE lot more! Living in your superpower helps you say no! As a young boss, it's hard to turn down business, or say no to new opportunities, but it's also vital to know your key strengths and play to them. ***There is power in saying no*** or passing the role to someone else who can actually do it faster or better than you.

With reference to the quadrant method (which I'll introduce shortly), I often find myself getting stuck in the "like it, but not good at it" box, and maybe you do too! I like to write emails and scripts and books, and writing comes pretty naturally to me, but when it comes time to write copy for sales emails or blogs, it takes me two to three times as long as my in-house copywriter. To say nothing about the fact that I'm notorious for sending out the email at the wrong time, to the wrong list, etc. So when I do it myself because I enjoy doing it, it not only takes me a long time, I'm robbing someone else of their role. To the point that the team had to metaphorically slap my hands and tell me to 'back off! They've got it!' It's a hard pill to swallow, but keeping tasks for yourself and not distributing the work appropriately stymies your team. Some team members will get lazy and end up relying on you to do their job, while others will feel underutilized and start resenting you and may start quietly quitting. Overall, knowing your strengths and living in them really helps your company to grow in a healthy way where everyone is in the right seats!

Chapter 10
FAKING IT

I don't know about you, but I am not into the idea of "faking it until you make it." It can lead to some terrible business practices. Now, there are certain times when you use that rule to gloss over minor things before you understand them completely, like an acronym here or there, but in life, this probably isn't a great rule to live by. Unpopular opinion, I know! But the truth is it can be dangerous. When you pretend you know what you're doing, you can hurt people in the long run. Let's say you got hired to run ads for a brand-new business. They've budgeted $30K, and they're expecting you to bring in 250 calls with that budget. You've agreed, but here's the problem: you don't know what you're doing! WELL YIKES! First, why would you have agreed to do it and taken their money?! Second, stop! It's going to be way more embarrassing to go back to them having failed than it would be to admit you're not qualified to do what they're asking and recommend someone else. They will respect you so much more for being transparent and honest and not wasting their money.

The reason I feel the need to bring up this topic is because, unfortunately, when it comes to many young bosses, they don't have the practice saying, "Sorry, that's outside of my scope." Their ego gets in the way, and it can be a huge downfall. It's a problem in our space, people who think they'll figure it out along the way. Sometimes you will, but what if you don't? If it's your own money on the line, that's different from someone else's time or money. So be cautious. I'm not saying to stay in your box and only do what you know, but I am saying to make sure you're not lying. ***If you don't know how to do something, become an expert, then come back and tackle it.***

It's far more trustworthy to be transparent about your current capabilities. Or take a tip from one of our YoungBoss Podcast guests, Jamila Stewart of Events by Jamila, and hire out someone else experienced underneath you to take that duty on. Yes, you'll get paid less, but the job will be done correctly, you can learn from them, and next time, you'll know what to do!

Chapter 11
SOLOPRENEUR VS TEAM

When it comes to growing your team from just you to many team members, there are quite a few things to consider, and the first is why. Start asking yourself WHY you're wanting or planning to add team members. Is it because you're overwhelmed and need help? Is it because you aren't living in your highest and best use? Is it because you have a vision of a large team of 100 or more people? Is it because you are lonely? I truly believe in the phrase "delegate and elevate" for my director and C-level positions, and especially my Visionaries. You are not the one who is meant to be DOING the work, but instead living in your superpower of being the idea man or woman, being the face, or bringing culture and people together for a purpose. Just like we talked about prior, knowing yourself and knowing your skills and weaknesses will aid you here. Hiring people to help and fill in those worker-bee tasks is vital. You are robbing someone of doing their God-given role when you try to be the end all, be all. You have to give up and release and find the right people to put into the right seats when it's time. Be cautious when you make this transition because, naturally, if you've been doing all the roles yourself and now you have to train someone else to do them, you're going to have moments where you want to take back over. It's like having kids, or so they say! You have to show them repeatedly and see them through mistakes, but eventually, they'll be doing it better than you ever did. During your first few weeks of training with a new person, you'll start to wonder why you brought them on in the first place when you could have done what they're slated to do yourself. That's when you need to remember your WHY. And this is also where timing comes into play.

The timing of hiring matters. Make sure you're not waiting until you are completely overwhelmed and then saying NOW. Now is when I need to bring someone on! That's probably the worst thing you could do because you're not setting them or yourself up for success. You won't have the time or energy to train them, which means it's going to take longer for them to get into the fold of the business and how you do things. You'll end up more frustrated because it's taking them so long, and you'll start questioning their talents and skills, when the reality is it just came down to timing. You didn't have the capacity to onboard them properly, and now the whole thing comes off the wheels! *When you're getting to that 75 to 80 percent capacity load, consider hiring someone!*

The way I create the job description is actually quite simple, and based on truly getting things off my plate that don't serve me or the company in the best way possible. Create a quadrant with four squares and label them the following:

1. Things I love to do and I'm good at
2. Things I like to do and I'm bad at
3. Things I don't like to do but I'm good at
4. Things I hate to do and I'm bad at

For most entrepreneurs, their box number one will be full, they will have a hard time filling box number two without someone telling them what's up, and boxes numbers three and four will have some things. This is where knowing yourself comes into play. Once you've made this quadrant, leave it on your desk for one to two weeks. During this time, you need to set a timer on your phone to go off every twenty to thirty minutes during your workday. Every time it goes off, whatever task you're doing at the time needs to go into one of these four boxes. Yes, this will add twenty minutes to your day, but it's the best way to get a job description down, I promise!

You'll realize you're doing a lot more than you think, and once you categorize something in the fourth quadrant (things I hate to do and I'm bad at), it becomes more important than ever to offload it officially. Once you feel you have a solid list of things, those boxes two to four are the new job description! You have to turn them into tasks and think about how you're going to train someone to do it the way you want, but truly, that's the first role. Get those things off your plate because as long as you're living in boxes two to four, you're not making the best use of your time or living in your superpower. You are stifling yourself and not bringing your company what it needs from you. It's time to change that! People often find these roles fall into maybe two different job descriptions, not just one, and that's okay. You can hire two people to help out. They may find other things that they can bring to the table you hadn't thought of yet. You also may find that the tasks or roles in these boxes have nothing to do with each other, and you are seemingly looking for a unicorn. If that happens, it's okay. We are going to focus on which ones are the MOST important to get off your plate first and turn those into a role, and then work from there. Many times, solopreneurs first hire for an assistant/catch-all type role because that's the truth of it. Look for the unicorn, but settle for the horse with the horn, and do the same quadrant exercise with them and yourself, a few years or months down the line. You'll see if there is anything more they can take off your plate and find what the next hire's role is going to look like. Continue building roles in this way, and you'll never overstaff or pay for things that are unnecessary or that someone internally could do exceptionally well.

I also want to note some people and businesses thrive in the solopreneur mode. Maybe you're in the beauty industry, and you don't want to build a big team. You want to stay just you, and you like it that way. You do the scheduling, the marketing, the appointments, the follow-up, the social media promotions, the payments, etc. There is nothing wrong with that at all. Most team growth comes from a vision. If that's not in your business plan, your vision, then don't let anyone pressure you. ***Being a solopreneur is a lot of fun because there is no one you have to answer to, or be responsible for, and you get to make every single decision on your own. Do what works for you!***

Chapter 12
IS THIS THE TOP?

Achieving so much at a young age can be scary, like… Did I peak? What if nothing you do after this is as good? What if this is it? DAMN, that's terrifying, but it's a common thought of many young bosses I've spoken with before. Like my friend, Sarah, who owns a tattoo shop. She didn't have anyone there to help her get started. She took out a loan on her own, purchased the building, and started tattooing. Barely making ends meet, she worked seven days a week, all day, every day. She gave up her social life and didn't date for four years because she seriously didn't have the time. The shop was her baby, and she gave it her all. Eventually, she got a couple more artists to come in and work under her, and now, four years later, she has fourteen employees and is running a super successful tattoo studio, making money like she never imagined. She got her social life back and started dating the love of her life. Her grit paid off in the end. But every night, she dreams that something happens, the studio shuts down, and she has to start over. What if she can't make it work? We chat about this topic often because I think it's totally normal to be hesitant and fear failure, thinking when is the other shoe going to drop? But the reality is we are all going to fail at some point, so why fear what is inevitable?

Failure isn't the end. I've met so many entrepreneurs who had to experience failure fifty times before they hit it big. It's part of the journey, and it's actually what makes success so much sweeter, knowing, at any turn, it may have NOT turned out that way. Like my dad, when he hit an egg in sales! I think the culture around failure has to change. We should embrace it instead of fearing it or running from it. If you've never failed, you've never really tried.

Besides, *if you've done it once, you can do it again.* We all have different journeys to success, but giving up can't be an option. Oprah was told she "wasn't a fit for TV." She didn't give up and look at Sis now. Walt Disney was fired from a newspaper for "lacking imagination and having no original ideas." Can you imagine if he gave up? Or Albert Einstein. He wasn't able to speak until he was almost four years old, and his teachers said he would "never amount to much." I don't know about you, but I have a lot of friends who have young children, and when these kids aren't starting to speak at one year old, the parents start to panic. Can you imagine having a four-year-old who can't speak?! You better believe Mr. and Mrs. Einstein thought something was majorly wrong! I mean, that's really concerning, and yet his name is synonymous with genius. If you're going to fail, fail big. Fail hard. Don't fear it. It's going to happen. Embrace it.

Chapter 13
EVERY DAY ABOVE GROUND IS A GREAT DAY

Sometimes being a young boss can be difficult. You are going to face many challenges, from firing to hiring, from having no capital and not knowing how you're going to keep the lights on, to making more money than you've ever wished and being terrified for tax season. There is so much you may face. But your attitude, your positivity, your perspective, your support group must be your shining light. As my favorite artist, Pitbull, says, "This is for everybody going through tough times, believe me, been there, done that. But every day above ground is a great day, remember that." It's true. There is nothing that will truly knock you out in business—and by that, I literally mean a failed business won't kill you. But please be cognizant that it can feel that way. The feeling that it can or will is very real, and many entrepreneurs face depression, anxiety, and thoughts of suicide more than most other careers.

Entrepreneur.com states, "Early-stage entrepreneurs may literally work alone—without team members or sounding boards. What's more, entrepreneurs tend to build professional networks more than close social circles (i.e., networks before friendships). Most potential confidants have touchpoints in the business world. It's often difficult to discuss deep vulnerabilities."[3] These factors lead to a propensity for negative feelings about success, your worth and value, and what you're doing here on this earth. We all can probably think of an entrepreneur who ended their life too soon because they felt they failed and had no one to go to, because they'd let everyone down. For example, I work with most of my family members: my mother, my sister, my brother and, at one point, also my ex-husband, his mother, and my sister- and brother-in-law. I mean, it's a lot! And to think that if I don't perform, if I don't sell, if I don't make the right decisions, no one eats. That's a lot of pressure. ***It's not about you as an entrepreneur or business owner. It's actually about everyone else.***

Oftentimes, business owners won't take a cut for the first few years because of this immense amount of pressure, constantly feeling like they can't win, even if they are winning. It can be a lot. Positivity isn't going to get you through everything, but it can help. In conjunction with building a strong network of friends and family members who you can talk to about your struggles and stresses, seek out a mastermind group to join or find a therapist. It's vital you don't go at this alone. You must build your protection. You must open yourself up to being vulnerable, even or especially if you're struggling with mental health. There are people who've gone before you, who've been through the same things, who are willing to help you push past and get through. There will be ups and downs, but having the support surrounding you really can help. And you must realize at the end of the day that, if you fail in your business, it's just one failure. It does not mean YOU are a failure. And that is OKAY! Being a young boss isn't made for everyone; you have to have grit tenfold. ***You have to be willing to get punched in the face and get back up over and over again.*** It is tough! But your mindset will protect you in those times of failure;

---

[3] Sherry Walling, "Entrepreneurs Could Be at a Higher Risk for Suicide. A Psychologist Explains Why," Entrepreneur, Sep. 4, 2022, https://www.entrepreneur.com/living/why-entrepreneurs-could-be-at-a-higher-risk-for-suicide/432083.

your positivity, your perspective will bring you through. It is not the end. It's the beginning. ***So change your perspective and save your life.***

Chapter 14
THE LONELY ISLAND

When you start on your entrepreneurial journey, you may be going at it alone, and that sucks. There might be people who don't believe in you, who say you're stupid or don't have the money, skills, or resources to get it done. HATERS! That's all they are, my friend! I have a piece of advice that I beg you to take. Get away from them! Run! They will not help you get to the top. They will not motivate, inspire, or encourage you! Surround yourself with people who want to see you win. I like to call those haters crabs because when you put more than one in a bucket, they pull each other back to the bottom, so no one can get out. This is what it's like to be in a relationship with someone who doesn't want to see you win. They're not pulling you down because they don't love you. They're pulling you down because they're scared that if you get out of the bucket, they'll be stuck at the bottom all alone! They may pretend like they want you to win, but when it comes down to it, you know deep down who has your back and who doesn't. Now, I'm not trying to break up friendships or relationships, but I am trying to help save you. Not everyone was meant for the journey of success. Not everyone understands it.

Even though I've encouraged you to run, I also suggest you have a deep, heavy, and hard conversation with your friends or family who are giving you this energy, to explain to them you want them there for the ride, but when they make comments like XYZ, it hurts you and actually makes you want to push them away. This conversation could be the catalyst for change and development in your friendships. Then they can grow with you, instead of apart from you. Voila! You've got a friend for life!

Maybe you had a supportive group of family and friends on your entrepreneurial journey, but once you started really winning, you felt alone. There is a reason people use the phrase, "It's lonely at the top." Because it is!

Grant Cardone is famously known for talking about how his wealth compounded the experience of loneliness. He said no one could go out on vacations with him. No one could ride in his private jet or spend the type of money he was looking to spend on dinners, etc. He realized he had to level up his friends. He wanted people with whom he could enjoy spending his life, time, and wealth.

I know leaving people behind seems sad and mean, but you're not leaving them. You're categorizing your life. I have friends who I will travel with because they like to spend the way I like to spend. I don't just mean money. I also mean time. My friends who don't have jobs they care about, or that ask a lot of them, get frustrated with me that at breakfast on vacation, I want to do a quick forty-five minute email check-in. But my friends who are more entrepreneurial are sitting there with their laptops doing the exact same thing. So I learned there are people you spend time with for different things, and that's okay. Take going out to dinner. That's one of my favorite things to do. A really nice restaurant with a great vibe and excellent service is one of my favorite ways to spend my money and extra time. Well, we all know those friends who say they didn't even eat the appetizers, or they only had one drink, so they want to split the check accordingly. RAWR! That's the worst! When I go out, we all order, eat, and enjoy, and we all pay evenly. It's about togetherness—the memories and the moments shared. It's not about how much money is to be spent or not spent.

And for some, I'M the WORST type of person to go to dinner with for exactly that reason! They want to only pay for what they ate, and it pisses them off to eat with someone who does it differently. You see, I'm not pushing away their friendship. I'm categorizing! And so are they! As a young boss, I suggest you do the same. Get friends who do what you like to do, whether it's boating, golfing, eating out, having spa days, or traveling. Find those people you can do those things with at your level, at your speed. Don't lose friends over it. Just categorize and keep on moving!

I mentioned not having friends or support in the beginning and the end, but what about in the middle too? When you're having serious struggles in your business, but all your friends work nine-to-five and don't relate, and you feel like you can't bring things up in front of them? That's lonely too. At some point in your entrepreneurial journey as a young boss, you're going to feel alone. I just want you to know it's normal. ***The best thing you can do is understand why they may abandon you or try to pull you down. Categorize your friendships and try to find a tribe who can relate to you.***

When it comes to finding a tribe, I suggest starting with masterminds! Find an amazing group, share your struggles, and know that they have got your back. It will change the game for sure. Also, let go of the guilt. Just because you are doing well, starting your own business, or becoming successful in your own realm doesn't mean you did, or are doing, anything wrong. It is not uncommon for young bosses to start putting themselves down in front of their friends and family because they don't want to be the shining star. So don't let that happen either. Be proud of the work you've done, but know where you can and can't open up. It's also okay to test and try to see if some people can relate, or have the mindset, that helps you continue in your growth. The worst that can happen is you share a struggle your business is going through with a non-business-owning friend or family member, and they don't understand and tell you, "Ya know, I think you should just quit. It sounds like this is the end, but you did really well, so don't worry. Lots of businesses fail every day. Maybe your next one will be the one." If they say that to you, but you were literally just working through one issue, the reality is they just don't understand. It's not about giving up or quitting. It's about working through it, and now you know this probably isn't the right person with whom to share your business struggles. AND THAT IS OKAY. Remember? Categorizing! They are still your family member or friend. They're just not in the inner circle of your business relationships. It's all good. You live and you learn!

Chapter 15
DUMBEST PERSON IN THE ROOM

One challenge that comes with being a young boss is getting into the right rooms. I genuinely believe being the dumbest person in the room is an ideal situation! It's vital to growing, but sometimes, just opening that door to get into that room can be tough. At times, people may not welcome you, whether because they're much older or because they're more experienced, but haven't shared your success. Joining masterminds and groups of like-minded people is a smart way to get involved with other entrepreneurs like yourself, but my biggest tip is to enter the room with humility. You are probably going to be the youngest person there already, so you don't need to lead with it. They can see for themselves. You also don't need to lead with your accomplishments and achievements. They know to just get into the room you've had to have done something big. There is a strange energy that can emerge when you're young and successful. It can either trigger older people, or it can encourage them to mentor you and scoop you up into their inner circle. Hopefully, you can find a group that tends to the latter angle. I've found that some mastermind groups are dick-measuring contests where it's all about whose numbers are better and who's selling the most, etc. By contrast, others foster the energy of comradery. They truly open doors for connections and intimacy. As they say, it can be lonely at the top. Surrounding yourself with others who know and understand the challenges that come with being a boss, whether young or old, can really aid in your devotion to your company, your idea, your why, your team, etc. Some of my favorite masterminds are the following:

Leadership Boardroom: https://www.leadershipboardroom.com/home

EO: https://hub.eonetwork.org

Family Mastermind: https://mattandrews.us

My best advice is to find your tribe, people who aren't threatened by you, people who are open and willing to share their vulnerable experiences. Find yourself a group where you can be yourself and get raw, sharing the hard times and the things with which you're struggling. With this said, note I'm not saying that you should find a therapist. I'm saying find people who have been through these things and can help guide you. They can come alongside you, encourage you, and give you resources and connections. They can follow up with you and make sure you're moving in a better direction.

When I meet a Boomer who owns a business and has a great group of core friends, or is a part of a club or mastermind of other business owners, they're almost ALWAYS more successful than Boomers who refuse to take advice and want to do it all on their own. I mean, none of these big entrepreneurs did it alone… they all had teams. Steve Jobs had a team, Mark Cuban has a team, Bethenny Frankel has a team—even Jesus had a team! **Having a team, a group of people you can call on, makes life worth living. It helps you excel; it helps push you.**

For me, the Leadership Boardroom has been one of the best experiences of my life. The leader of the group, Shaun McCloskey, welcomed me with open arms. During my interview to enter the group, I had to share my experiences, my stats, my wins and losses, and get really real with him. He became my biggest advocate and fan. It felt good to have someone with whom to share my wins. Oftentimes, as entrepreneurs, we are terrible at celebrating our wins, and Shaun really let me revel in my success.

During my first group meeting, he had me sit back and observe a little. The format of the meeting was the following: one person shared something they were struggling with, personal or professional, and everyone went around and gave insight and helpful tips or questions to poke holes, etc. It's a private group, and nothing is shared outside the room, so it allows people to get really vulnerable, and that's a beautiful thing, especially in business where we're rarely encouraged to be open.

The first person who shared really set the tone. They poured their heart out, sharing some deep-rooted issues that were ruining their culture. Everyone offered insights to help resolve the issues. Shaun let everyone speak, and when it seemed like it was coming to a close, he turned to me, and knowing that my favorite topic in the world is company culture, he asked, "So do you have any insight?" I walked into this room humble, ready to listen, soak up, and learn. My intention was not to wow anyone with my background or insight, but I started to give them some food for thought. I shared some personal struggles we had to face within our culture and how we overcame them. I gave them some tools they could use to help overcome the problems and recommended some books for their team, amongst other things. The whole room was quiet, and finally, one guy said, "Well, gosh, why didn't you go first?!" We all broke into laughter, and it lightened the mood a lot!

I then felt free to share during almost everyone else's turn. Over that weekend, I developed such a strong bond with this amazing group of individuals. It was beyond refreshing having others to go to for tough things. It was exactly what I needed.

This type of group is important for things you may not want to admit to others, even your spouse or partner. Even better, they really focus on your vision. One of the first things you do is set your vision plan for your life, business, etc. Before you enter the room, the entire group has read and understands your vision, so when you bring up issues, they revert back to your dreams and goals in your vision. They help keep you on track! Post-event, everyone in the group reached out to me individually to check in, say hello, and see how things were developing. They became my Board of Advisors, my friends, my family, and my confidants. In business and life, it's important to have that group, and unfortunately, your friends who are working nine-to-five, or don't have your same ambitions, simply can't understand oftentimes. Surrounding yourself with people who get it, who want to help, and who have more experience than you is a major key.

As Proverbs 11:14 says, "For lack of guidance a nation falls, but victory is won through many advisors." (NIV) I highly suggest checking out one of these groups or another one in your area as a place for you to let your hair down and take off the armor of being the person at the top. Lock yourself into this place of friendship and respite. ***Take what you need and give what you can.*** This is your tribe, your people, and for that, you can be ever so open, vulnerable, and honest.

Chapter 16
CELEBRATE GOOD TIMES, COME ON!

One major lesson I learned from the Leadership Boardroom was celebrating my wins! As entrepreneurs and young bosses, we often get caught up in the climb and forget to look down and see how far we've come. For example, my first time selling $1,000,000 from the stage, my team sent bottles of champagne to my house and congratulatory flowers, etc. And I took the bottle… and put it away.

LIKE WHYYYYY!?!?! Why didn't I celebrate at that moment!?

Why didn't I grab that bottle, pop the top, spray it everywhere, and dance in my joy?

I didn't even know how to celebrate that win. All my thoughts and worries were going to whatever was next. I didn't cheer. I didn't dance. I didn't drink or block the next day off from work. Back to normal operations. And I'm not alone. So many young bosses just love the climb so much that it's hard for us to stop and smell the roses. Whenever I spoke to someone in my mastermind group and they inevitably asked how I celebrated my wins, they were like WTF when they heard me say it was business as usual. And rightfully so! I mean, let's be real. Why are we even working so hard, why are we pushing to accomplish so much, if we aren't going to soak up the moments when we actually get there?! If we aren't going to scream and shout and celebrate like

Shaq winning the Triple Crown! Come on! So I encourage you to do the following:

A. Find people to celebrate your win with you. Ask them to support you in it. Ask them to remind you to celebrate and to be there for you when you do.

B. Make a list of what a celebration looks like! That way, you actually know what you're doing, and you don't just fall into it.

My list included booking a spa day. Blocking out the following day of work and spending it in nature or with my dog. Going to a super-expensive dinner. Buying myself a new piece of jewelry. And booking a vacation. Whatever yours looks like is fine. You have to pick things that genuinely excite you and give you a moment of joy! Lastly, you must, must, ***must be IN the moment when you're celebrating!*** You can't just celebrate one foot in and one foot out. It has to be all in! Shut off your phone, shut off yourself from the world, and be in it. Be the winner. Being present is key for a true celebration!

I can also guarantee the moment you start celebrating is the moment you start enjoying your wins. Prior to the celebration, I didn't even enjoy hitting goals because it didn't change anything. It all felt the same. Now, I love reaching new goals, and I am lighter and happier when I do! I can't wait to accomplish things because those celebrations are everything!

Chapter 17
DO YOU HEAR WHAT I HEAR?

Wanna know the biggest secret to being a great young boss? Listening. There is nothing more impactful you can do with your staff, your clients, and your competition than listening when it comes to business. Listening does not necessarily mean doing what they are suggesting, but it does mean being willing and open to hearing it. People want to be heard, and **often, your team will have excellent insight into matters that you don't see or understand yet.** And when it comes to them, always make sure they know you heard them. The worst thing is when you have a boss who doesn't seem to care about your ideas.

We had an incredible staff member who has been bringing one particular idea up for almost two-and-a-half years. Each time he brought it up, I made sure he knew I heard him, acknowledged that we did need to implement that idea, and that I really did agree with him. At the same time, I'd make clear to him that the timing wasn't right because we had other things that were more important, or the money wasn't there yet. All the reasons I gave him were true! I loved his insight and idea and wanted to bring it to fruition, but it really wasn't the time yet. The wonderful thing is that because I acknowledged, leaned in, even took some meetings on the idea, and explained exactly why we couldn't now, he was never upset when his idea wasn't chosen. He completely trusted us because we listened. So just a few weeks ago, we had a team meeting, and it was finally time to implement the idea. I shared with the team that Matt had been bringing up an excellent idea for some time, and we wanted to thank him for his persistence! It was time to bring it to life, and that we did! He was grateful to us for continuing to keep it in mind, and we were thankful for the idea.

Now, on the other hand, sometimes your staff will bring you ideas that you will listen to, but will not want to implement. That is okay. It's all about making sure they know you heard them and care. Another staff member has continuously brought up a particular topic and suggestion. At first, we thanked him, let him know we heard him, and reassured we would follow up. When we did follow up, it was about the budget. We told him that constraints would not allow for this suggestion to come to fruition. We gave a full and clear explanation, so when this particular team member brought the idea up again, we had already explained why it wouldn't happen. Even so, he didn't feel heard. I took another one-on-one meeting and asked him to explain his suggestion in more detail. I also asked if he remembered our call and reasoning as to why we opted to not go this direction. He could recall the conversation, but thought he would try again. We all have team members like this sometimes. He really pushed on how this would be best for everyone overall, so I asked if he would be willing to take a pay cut to make it happen, and he said no. At that point, I think it finally hit him. If it wasn't worth it to him financially to take the hit, why would it be worth it to the business, unless it was going to bring in more money? But it wasn't, and he finally understood. He thanked me for the one-on-one and never brought it up again. Active listening is vital with your staff.

Our phone sales team kept bringing up the process of follow-up, asking if we could automate it, because I am not on the phones like they are day to day. I did not see the problem as they described it. I asked if I could come shadow them for one day, and they, of course, accepted the offer. After being in their shoes for four hours, I realized the follow-up process was extending their off-the-phone time, and if they had an automated system, they could all fit an additional three calls into their day. Three calls times six people was quite a bit of money being left on the table. I put in a work order to automate their follow-up system immediately. They felt heard and loved having me there to watch them work. In turn, I grew in appreciation for them. Our communication was stronger as a result of this interaction because they were willing to ask, which can be a scary thing sometimes! I was willing to listen to the fullest extent and put myself in their shoes. And we took action together. Being open to listening will change the way your staff approaches you.

When it comes to clients, listening is also vital. Asking for feedback and hearing what they say—the good, bad and ugly—is what you need to move forward and make improvements. No one knows better than the people paying for your services. Clients may give harsh truths, but it's important not to brush them off. If they're complaining about the food options you're giving them, listen. If they're saying they expected higher-quality materials, listen. If they're saying you're boring when you get up on stage, listen. Of course, there is always going to be someone in the crowd you cannot please. As they say, 10 percent of a room will never buy. But being able to truly listen, and possibly upgrade or change the way you do things based on client feedback, is everything.

Lastly, I encourage you to **listen to your competition.** See what they are doing better or worse than you. Listen to what makes them unique. It's not just what makes them unique is good either. Sometimes customers will dislike them for that very reason. Then you know you can bring those people in by highlighting and marketing what the other company is not. I am not a fan of copying or imitating, but I will say that we have a competitor who copies our every move, and it serves him well. When we post a video on YouTube, he gets it transcribed, and within one to two weeks, he will post the exact same video with our exact same words, changing out his name and the name of his company, of course. It's insane. It truly is, BUT here's the thing. The way he delivers the message is different. I'm a thirty-something-year-old white female, and he's a sixty-something-year-old black man. Our approach, tonality, and linguistics are very different. Even though my team and I can see the similarities in what we are saying, it's presented differently so the consumers cannot tell the difference. Some people love him and hate me, and vice versa. That is okay. I am listening. My ears are open. My competition is telling me I am the best. They're copying my every word, for goodness' sake! They can't even come up with their own creative content, but it doesn't matter. What matters is that I listen to the customer through the eyes of the competition. Some people will never like you, and that's okay. Listen to what they do like, and if it's authentic to you, add it. If it's not, avoid it like the plague.

Chapter 18
EGOTISTICAL MANIAC

Ego and business are far too often found in the same room, especially with young business owners and entrepreneurs. It makes me really sick when I meet another young boss, and they are completely full of themselves. It's like, come on, tone it down for all of us, please!!! We get it. You're awesome, and you've accomplished some great things, and I definitely think you should be proud of yourself, but being confident and proud are not the same as being an egotistical maniac! Far too often, young bosses get full of themselves after a little success, but what goes up must come down. When you talk to older people who've been in business awhile, they'll always tell you it's not all peaches and cream. They've hit the bottom hard! "According to the U.S. Bureau of Labor Statistics (BLS), this isn't necessarily true. Data from the BLS shows that approximately 20 percent of new businesses fail during the first two years of being open, 45 percent during the first five years, and 65 percent during the first 10 years. Only 25 percent of new businesses make it to 15 years or more."[4] OUCH! But guess what? Most of these older bosses did something different. They got back up!

We can take heed of their grit and determination. That's all a part of the journey. So don't think just because you made it big once means

---

[4] Michael T. Deane, "Top 6 Reasons New Businesses Fail," Investopedia, Dec. 30, 2022, https://www.investopedia.com/financial-edge/1010/top-6-reasons-new-businesses-fail.aspx.

you're hot shit! At some point you may become actual shit and have to reframe and rebuild it all.

The smartest thing a young boss can do is play it cool, remain humble, and look for opportunities to learn. Remember, you want to be the dumbest person in the room, not the opposite. This is important because it will literally aid you in retaining more business and building a stronger reputation and brand! When you enter a room thinking you're God's gift to earth, no one in that room thinks they can help you or be of service to you. After all, you've got it all figured out, right?! But on the other hand, ***when you enter a room, and you're humble and share both your successes and failures, people see an authentic soul, and they want to reach out for feedback, networking, and connections.*** Sometimes their advice could help launch you to the next level. I operate a multimillion-dollar real estate seminar business, and I've taken advice from people who have never spoken on stage and don't own real estate at all because what they had to say was right, and I was open to hearing their reasoning! If I led with ego, I would have dismissed their feedback and been in a worse place. It all starts with being open.

I'll never forget one time I was sharing with my nine-year-old niece about a new app we were building. I was excited thinking I had thought through every single angle, and I was going to really hit it big with this new idea! She is wicked smart and loves hearing about new inventions, but obviously has no business experience. She simply said to me, "And you're going to make it so other business owners could use it too?"

I turned to look at her like, "Huh?" She was referring to white-labeling the product without having the knowledge of the proper lingo, but she saw something I didn't. I was focused on my clients, my students, and not thinking of applications outside of our business. A nine-year-old… come on, people! No, I hadn't thought of that yet. But like duh! Of course, we should! This specific app could be rebuilt for anyone in the info space who teaches different step-by-step programs for real estate investing, or really any type of investing. She wasn't being facetious, and she wasn't being rude; she was simply suggesting something I probably should have thought of and didn't. I could have dismissed her completely, as she is a child. But instead, I thanked her for her idea and encouraged her by saying, "Ya know, that's an amazing idea I didn't think of! You are incredibly smart to think of that. Thank you for the idea! I will definitely go back to the drawing board to make sure we include it. Thank you."

Out of the mouths of children come fabulous ideas! If I was an egotistical maniac, I could have been threatened, I could have been dismissive and told her she didn't get my vision. I could have done a million things! But leading with humility, I understood she, a small child, could even bring ideas to the table. And guess what? We did end up white-labeling it, and IT IS bringing in a lot of money. She deserves a cut!

Or that time when my sister-in-law wasn't working with me yet, and she was just my brother's girlfriend attending a work event with us. I needed extra hands on deck, so I asked her to jump in. She is an absolute rockstar, but I didn't know that yet. I just saw her for what she was to me at the time, my brother's girlfriend who worked at Starbucks and was with us on this trip. Well, during her day with me, she started throwing out suggestions on how to do things faster, less manually, more automated. At first, I was a bit annoyed. I had been running the show for three years at this point, and I felt very defensive, almost like, "Come on, girl. Just help me do the work and shut up! If you keep coming up with these ideas on how to 'improve' all my processes, I'm going to be annoyed and tell you to just go back inside, sit in the class, and not help." My ego was flaring up, and I could feel it. Instead of diving into those negative thoughts, I was so overwhelmed at this particular event, I turned to her and said, "If you think that idea will help us do this task better, let's go for it! You lead the way. Show me what you're thinking." And we did it her way. Guess what!? It was WAY better than the way I was doing it. The task went from taking me fifteen minutes to about two minutes, and it freed up more time for me to do the other million tasks we needed to accomplish that day. Yes, a Starbucks barista dating my brother knew better than me. DAMN. That hit me right in the chest! From that moment forward, I trusted her more. While some of her ideas were not home runs, many of them were excellent, and we eventually ended up hiring her on as our full-time Operations Director the following year. ***Staying humble will literally help you do things faster and better. It will also leave room for more financial opportunities,*** and we all know that's vital in running a business.

Chapter 19
YOU'RE FIRED

Ouch! For me, firing people has been one of the worst parts of my job. Now, for some young bosses, an HR department can remove this responsibility from your life, but for most who are starting out, especially in the beginning, this is something you're going to have to do yourself. Both hiring and firing can be tricky, bittersweet, exciting, and heartbreaking. I've had to fire my brother, sister-in-law, mother-in-law, cousins, friends, and even my ex-husband. Talk about tough! Whether it's someone you barely know, someone you don't like, or someone you love and will see every day for the rest of your life, firing is always a challenge. During these conversations, make sure you:

1. Always have offenses and reasons documented. You cannot fire someone on a whim. If they have signed a contract that has listed clearly fireable offenses, use it. If you're writing them up for each offense instead of just having a conversation, this will also work. Put simply, you need proof. Many young bosses get into trouble here. They only have conversations and don't document. When it's time to let someone go, there's no legitimate reason, so the person feels blindsided and fires back.

2. Make sure you go about it with tact. Do not get overly emotional. Stay calm in the conversation, make sure it's recorded, and ensure someone else is there—maybe an HR head or someone on your team at a high level. It helps eliminate "he said/she said" type scenarios.

3. Be kind. It's never fun to be let go from a job. Remember this and think about what they might be going through. Give them grace, understanding, and honesty. Understand that keeping someone in a job when they aren't performing is actually hurting them. As a boss, it's better for you to let them go where they can find a role and thrive, instead of drowning at your company.

Almost each and every time I have fired someone, I felt terrible. My heart broke, and I immediately regretted it, thinking, *What if I tried harder? What if I put them in a different role? What if I didn't support them enough?* But the truth is I did try hard, and so did they, probably. I did try multiple roles or positions. I did support them. I gave it my all. So genuinely, it just wasn't a right fit. And that's okay. Every person I've ever let go has found another role. They're all doing A-OK! All of them are thriving. PHEW!

Just remember they're going through a lot. I've had people laugh at me, cry, scream, or be silent, and a few were extremely kind and humble throughout. It's all over the place. Emotions are a funny thing like that. **Being fired sucks. And firing someone sucks, too! Stay calm, be kind, and remember that at one point you were stoked to hire this person.** They do have incredible skills; they're just not able to execute them in the way you need at this time in your company, OR they aren't a culture or core value fit. The hard truth is they will be all those things for someone else, just not you!

Chapter 20
I QUIT

Have you heard about this craze called quiet quitting? It's when someone starts to slowly back away from you, the company, and their role. You can almost sense when they go home they're looking for something new or different. Sometimes they don't even want to go elsewhere; they just don't want to be where they are now. To me, this is such a tough one. When someone is checked out, it's not like they're doing anything particularly wrong, so it's tough to pinpoint. Having deep conversations with your staff about their happiness can at least make it apparent. If someone can do their job, but mentally be on Mars, is that okay with you? If so, it's nothing to concern yourself with. If not, this is a big stressor. You have to make sure people feel bought in. It could be nothing to do with you and more to do with the role, but regardless, quiet quitting is like death by a thousand cuts. It's a long process that culminates in a difficult choice. To let them stay or let them go. My suggestion ***is always to let them go. They'll be happier elsewhere, and you'll be happier not stressing about their happiness or fulfillment at your company***. Delivering bad news builds trust. Be honest, open, and transparent about what you're seeing.

When you have someone who actively and openly quits on you, this is a major learning lesson time as a young boss! I mean, think about it—someone is saying something, very loud about you or your business. Of course, there could be other reasons they're quitting, like moving, having a baby, etc. But if it's not a positive reason, then it's time to perk up! Have open and honest conversations with them about what went wrong and how they're feeling. Not promising but asking if there is anything you could have done to fix or change the situation. Or maybe it didn't have to do with you, per se, but someone who is a direct manager over them... what's the situation and details? It's time to dive in and find out how you can fix this issue from affecting others on the team.

Note that anytime someone is fired or quits, it gives a sense of uncertainty to the business at large. When someone is fired, the employees or independent contractors start to think... *Am I next?* And worry about what they've been doing right or wrong. When someone quits, oftentimes the boss starts to think, *Is everyone else going to quit? What don't I know about? What happened? Has it affected the others?*

Finding out those answers can save your company culture, so make sure to take the time to dive in and really determine if this situation was something that could have been saved.

Chapter 21
WELCOME NEWBIES

Hiring someone can be an incredibly fun, scary, and exciting time for a young boss. There may be a lot riding on this hire depending on if it's your first or your fiftieth! It's different each time! Make sure you have the role clearly laid out, and the training requirements, along with the Predictive Index cast for what you need as the first steps. Then check that they're a fit for the role and a fit for the company.

Hiring is such an important part of being a business owner because **one wrong hire can cost you a lot of money, time, resources, and stress**. I love having systems in place to help avoid any of those costs. A recommended reading before you hire anyone is a book called *A CEO Only Does Three Things: Finding Your Focus in the C-Suite* by Trey Taylor. In this book, you will start to learn and understand YOUR role within the company and the three things you need to focus on. Guess what? It's NOT what you might think it is. Many solopreneurs focus on doing a lot of the work themselves. But you can't forget to delegate and elevate! For example, my amazing young boss friend Brandon is a rockstar in his field. He's amongst the 7 percent of black-owned businesses, and he's a young boss, just like us! Brandon started his janitorial and maintenance business during COVID when he had more downtime than ever before. No time is better than the present, he figured. Since it was during a strange time in business, he was doing most of the work himself, and slowly, over the course of the next two years, he hired more and more key players so he could step away a bit. One day, he and I were chatting about his endgame goals, and he said, "I told myself I was just going to grind it out for three years." In reality, it had been four, and he was still doing daily tasks that the owner of a successful business had no business doing! I challenged him to read this recommended book, and we spoke after he did. He said, "Damn, Belle… You just really changed my perspective on my role within the company, and I've got to start hiring out more. It's time to work ON the business, not IN it. I'm fooling myself by saying one more year, one more month, one more anything. Time to hire and focus on my key players!" Remember, know yourself, your skills, and your limitations!

Here's a cheat sheet. The three things a CEO should do are focus on culture, people, and numbers. When you do all the other work yourself, you cannot build a strong culture because you're distracted. You cannot hire the right people because you feel you'd do it better yourself instead of investing IN them and empowering them. And lastly numbers. Now you may think working IN your business helps your numbers. But, reality check, it doesn't! When you're in the business, you think you're saving by not paying someone else or paying yourself less than what you'd pay someone else. First, that means you're falsely in the black. Second, that means you're tied up, and you can't focus on expansion, aka making MORE money! ***A CEO needs only to focus on those three things, and that will drive more business, more loyalty from employees, and more joy from yourself.*** I promise!

Now, once you find some candidates who may work, it's time to interview, asking questions this person has to think about. For example, emphasize value-based questions rather than vacuous questions like, "If you were a cereal, what cereal would you be?" We aren't GoDaddy, and we don't care, do we? At the end of the day, we want this person to blend well with the teammates they'll be working beside. We want them to complete their tasks, lead their team, or generate the sales we are seeking. We want a hard worker, someone we can rely on and trust, someone who will put the company first, and honor you as their boss, but also themselves as a representative for the company. All of these things are not too much to ask.

If you have a tight-knit team that this new person will be joining, after you've interviewed and narrowed down your candidates, I highly suggest you bring in the team to chat with this person one-on-one or as a group. They need to get to know them and feel out if they like them and can trust them. I have learned this the hard way. The team, especially when close, sometimes rejects a new person when they aren't involved in the onboarding and hiring process. Learn from me and incorporate them in those interviews. They sometimes can see things you cannot, and you'll want to know that before you invest a bunch of time, energy, money, and resources into this person, only to hear later on that they hate them and don't want to work with them… trust!

Once you and the team have chosen your new employee, onboarding begins! During this phase, you still need to be involved. You cannot throw this person to the wolves, no matter how much experience they have. They've never worked for you or your company. You must be by their side figuratively, or literally if you work in person, and show them how things are done. **It's much easier to train someone by showing them rather than explaining to them.** Let them see you, or their teammates, do things. Let them practice while being overseen and corrected or complimented after. Then they are open to do things on their own. One time, we hired what I thought would be a total rockstar. Her résumé and past experience were top-notch, and she came highly recommended. As a result, I jumped past a lot of what was described above. I didn't make her take the PI test. I didn't have the team interview her. I took the interview and hired. Quickly. Big mistake number one.

Unfortunately, her core values did not match ours. She was very corporate and had a strict outline of how things ought to go, which was very different from how things ran in our company. I did not bring her on to change the way things were done but, instead, to oversee them. She was a big personality and within three months had rubbed almost every single one of my team members the wrong way. She completely micromanaged every single one of them and made them feel like their work wasn't up to par, when they needed very little oversight, and their work was excellent. I kept telling them how capable she was and how she had this amazing background. They kept telling me she was… well, the worst! They told me she had no loyalty to me or the team. She was sneaky and snarky and constantly trying to trigger them. She made them feel like they weren't working hard enough so she could come back to me as the hero. I didn't see what they saw. I heard them, and I listened, and I tried my best to bring everyone back together. But we had a moment of breakthrough when we were asked to do the trust scale with one of our business coaches. Every one of them voted her 1, 2, or 3 out of 10 on how much they trusted her with her communication, character, consistency, commitment, caring, confidence, and competency. DAMN. I couldn't look away from this issue, and I had to make a move. We ended up firing this person, and it was a hard day. During her exit interview, she presented herself with anger. She tore down the others she was working for, dismissing their complaints, and said that she was better than all of them. She even went as far to say, "Really, you're going to choose a girl who used to work at In-N-Out over me!? WOW!" The reality is the girl who, yes, used to work at In-N-Out is one of my absolute best team members. Her loyalty is unmatched; her heart is for the company. She treats every single customer like gold. She bends over backwards for me, my family, our team, and the company at large. She is the true rockstar and guess what? In-N-Out taught her most of those skills! So yes, I will choose my burger-flipping queen all day over someone who is overqualified with a snotty attitude looking down upon our affiliates, customers, and team members.

That same year, we brought on another gal, with an incredible background as well, who I did ask to take the Predictive Index. I also let the team interview her, and I asked all the right culture and interview questions. She has proven to be an absolute killer in the workplace. The entire team loves and respects her. They brought her into the fold almost immediately. She has made it a point to meet with everyone one-on-one and feel them out, get to know them, and what they do, and see if she can help make any of their daily processes smoother by adding automation. We refer to her as the automation queen! She has taken each department and helped transform their daily tasks into a much simpler regimen. She is beloved by all and respected by many in and out of our industry. We are blessed to have her on board. I truly believe having the team buy in up front makes all the difference. At the end of the day, core values and culture are the biggest pieces of it all. Someone can do their job, but be a total bummer to hang out with, and that's not someone you want to bring into the fold. After all, **we spend most of our days and time at work. It should be a place we enjoy.**

Chapter 22
LET'S HEAR IT FOR THE GIRLS

What do I have to say about being a woman in business? Oh, Lord, where do we begin!? For some of my young bosses, you're already in a predominately woman-focused industry like lashes, permanent makeup tattoos, med spa, etc. And for those of you who are women running a woman-owned business serving primarily women, these issues may or may not apply to you. That's okay. You have something sacred that we women need: a place, a company, a business that serves as a respite from a male-dominated world. Now, I am not a man-hater by any means, but I would say that being a woman in a male-dominated industry comes with its challenges… and perks. Let's dig in.

One of the main challenges is being underestimated. Once I met an incredible woman who was in a male-dominated field, and she was a total rockstar, a killer. Everyone took her seriously… how did she do this? How could she gain the respect and love of these dominant men? She lived in her masculinity…at work. She was a force to be reckoned with. I see this trend with many women in male-dominated fields. They are oftentimes living in their masculine energy, and when they do, men respect them. They don't come at them as only sexual beings, but as people to work with and beside. It's very sad and hard, but I often have seen that when women live in their femininity at work, they are underestimated, overlooked, and oftentimes not taken seriously in the business world of mixed sexes. It's an unpopular opinion, but **when you're in a male-dominated field, it's okay to put your masculine energy forward and first. You have to be strong and domineering, and you can't take no for an answer.** The moment they see a place of vulnerability is the moment they think they've won. It's important to be strong, and I truly believe there is power in being a masculine female. Not to say that women are not strong or powerful—trust and believe I know we are the MOST powerful of all—but at work, it's not always interpreted that way. I understand these statements are not 100 percent true all the time. I'm just sharing what has worked for me and many other women in male-dominated fields. I am also not suggesting you live in your masculinity 100 percent of the time. At home, I am in my feminine power all day! But at work, it calls for a different side of me, a more balanced, but masculine-leaning side. I also think that is okay! It's okay to be balanced! But what really matters is resting on the knowledge that you deserve to be in the room. You have a spot, and you can be a benefit to others with your expertise and insight as much as they can benefit from you. Rest in your power, be who YOU are, and don't force anything. Show up authentically, no matter what that looks or feels like. If you are able to use the balance, do it. Practice it. You may find a lot of power and strength in it, and if it doesn't work for you, then keep doing your thing, queen! Whatever works for you in your field, and truly, you know best.

Whenever I'm invited to women-only events, unfortunately, it seems they are always behind the times. It sucks! It seriously does, but many women in business aren't in the same league as the men, and I know that's for many different reasons like lack of education on topics such as finance, investing, and strategy. But it's also because many of them took years off their careers to raise children. Today, 40 percent of entrepreneurs are women, which is at an all-time high. That is what makes it all the more wild to see that impact, but I think it makes women beasts in business for being so behind and disadvantaged. We understand *we are the underdogs, and we have the strength and power to say, "I get it, and I'm ready to work ten times harder. No challenge is too big."* But we also need to step up our game on financial literacy for young girls. It's time to level the playing field.

I know that my podcast, The YoungBoss Podcast, is a small start to trying to shape and change the way our community feels about female or younger entrepreneurs, but there are so many things to be learned. Some incredible companies or resources to teach girls about entrepreneurship and financial literacy are BrightChamps or Juni Learning! But let's be real. As hard as they try, the courses are still filled with more young boys than girls, and it's an issue. We need to change the way we educate young girls and encourage them to take part just like the boys do. It starts at home. It's our responsibility to do our part!

Watch out, though. The work culture is changing, and it's changing fast! We have more dominating women in every single field, and they are crushing it. Women are natural empaths. They listen to their staff and customers; they seek advice and are willing to make adjustments. But first and foremost, they are absolutely incredible young bosses.

The day I realized this was the day I recognized that most of my staff appreciated working for a woman. Some men in my company were grateful that I gave them time to be with their wives when they had COVID. They appreciated my willingness to give them much-deserved time at home after they had a baby. It even showed up in smaller ways, like spending quality time with them on work trips, listening to their life and work issues. I call this the in between. It's striking a balance between the masculine and feminine. When I'm with my staff, I'm able to bring both, and it's a beautiful thing, knowing and loving that precious combination of who you are and who you need to be!

There are some times in business that call for masculine energy and others that require you to be soft and sweet. It's the balance that truly makes us successful women in business. I will add a word of caution, though. Being a woman in business can be a blessing. You may be the only woman in the room. This often happens to me. At first it can be alarming. Then, when you put your walls down, you realize you have something none of them do! And I'm not just talking about private parts!

Men in general lean toward women. When there is a woman in the room, especially a young female boss, they want to know what got you there, who let you in, and why. Their questions may be condescending, and their comments may be unintentionally rude, but at the end of the day, you're the most popular person in the room. Networking is a breeze because everyone wants to be your friend, know your story, and hear what you have to say. Take advantage! You may not always have this edge, but use it where you can! Be the only woman, and present yourself with respect and kindness, showcasing all of your talents, wins, and abilities, winning those contracts and clients. You have the edge. Go for it, girl!

Chapter 23
IS IT ME OR IS THIS AMAZING!?

When it comes to running my own business, I feel like the luckiest girl in the world. I don't know about you, young boss, but for me? Oh yeah, baby! It's incredible. I am so grateful for the opportunity I have to work for myself on projects I'm excited about, surrounded by people I relish, and having experiences no one can take from me. There is this hilarious meme that says, "My boss arrived at work in a brand-new Lamborghini. I said, 'Wow, that's an amazing car!' He replied, 'If you work hard, put in all your hours, and strive for excellence, I'll get another one next year.'"

This is what working in corporate America does to people. It has you working day in and day out in service to someone else's dream. Whenever one of my friends comes to me and says, "I really think I could run a bachelorette party planning business," or, "My dream would be to open a make-it-yourself charcuterie store," I am beyond excited for them. I start making business plans, poking holes, and thinking of price points. I'm ready to start and support them immediately. Then inevitably, a little thing called doubt creeps into their minds. But the truth is working for someone else isn't a safer bet. You are only valuable to them if you're bringing in money or customer experiences. The moment you stop, slack, or they're overstaffed, you're gone. And that's a harsh reality to face! When you work for yourself, you control your destiny, you control the money in and out, and you get to make the decisions. Yes, that's a lot of pressure, but I think it's the best part of my job. I love that it all comes back to me. It's the most pressure you can imagine, and I say that from the perspective of running not just a business, but a family business. If I don't perform, if I don't make the right decisions, not only do thirty other people not eat, but my own mother, sister, and brother don't! That's an undeniable pressure. That's "can't eat, can't sleep, grinding your teeth at night" scary pressure. But it's what drives me! If you're a young boss like me, you know this is **the ONLY way to play in the game of life. This is the best way to control your income, live to your true potential, and become the highest and best version of yourself.**

It's terrifying to quit your ostensibly secure job, but eventually, you're going to have to do it if you want to bet on yourself. I am blessed that I grew up with an entrepreneurial father, and I know not everyone reading this has had that experience. Maybe your parents worked for the man, and they encouraged you to do the same. And if you were to step out on your own, they may be upset or disappointed in you. Family pressure is real. Partner pressure is real. I get it. But if you have the calling in your heart to create something on your own, you must. Sometimes that looks like staying at your corporate nine-to-five until you've saved up enough income or paid time off, or until you're at your wit's end. Sometimes it means working overtime, like my beautiful friend Anne. She is a writer and incredibly talented when it comes to fashion, styling, and the textile world. She's been working for a big company, and they run on East Coast hours. This is helping her launch her own business because she works for them from 6:00 a.m. to 3:00 p.m. MST, and then after 3:00, she gets time to work on her own stuff until 5:00 or 6:00 p.m. It's not a lot, but it's something. The big company pays the bills, and she is slowly chipping away at starting her own thing. *You've got to start somewhere, even if it's small!* Why is this important, you may ask? Because there are millions of people in the world with ideas, but you're one of the few who make ideas come to fruition. Staying motivated and excited isn't always easy. But don't let anyone tell you it's silly or unfathomable. It's not. It's 100 percent not. They say thoughtful individuals can't change the world, yet they're the only ones who ever have. Start today. Begin with the end in mind. Make room for it. Your dreams will become reality if you give them the attention and dedication they deserve.

Chapter 24
PROFESSIONALISM

Nothing could be more important as a young boss than having professionalism in all you do. This is so vital because—let's be real—we are YOUNG bosses, and sometimes, people don't take us seriously! So, to eliminate any haters from saying you don't dress or act the part, you can do some small things that really help even the playing field and make others, especially your seniors, respect you! For me, that looks like dressing the part, behaving the part, and staying true to myself. If you're a young boss who's under thirty, this can be really, really hard! It can seem unfair. All your other friends may post pictures in their bikinis or drink on the weekends. However, as a young boss, you may not actually do those things, but you definitely do not post about them.

Why is life so different for you? It's because—reality check—you're in a different league. Now, some people make it their brand to be partying or traveling all the time, and if that's your business brand, then do your thing, young boss! But if your clientele is much older than you, or much more conservative than you, it's important to stay professional. Most of my clients are business owners and operators, over twenty years my senior. They don't mind that I am younger, but I'm not leading with it. I'm not wearing ripped jeans or crop tops when I speak in front of them because that's not what they were taught is professional. Know your audience. They were taught (depending on where they grew up) to wear clothes that fit just right. While it's different from my generation's style choices, it's not a problem. You have all the rest of your life to wear hoodies and Jordans! I can put on a nice suit and dress the part for a speaking engagement to appease the audience. Because when you look professional, you remove some skepticism in the room. As Deion Sanders says, "If you look good, you feel good. If you feel good, you play good. If you play good, they pay good." They aren't distracted by what you're wearing. They aren't thinking about it. Instead, they're hearing and seeing you. That's the goal anyway, right!?

But there's something else I want to emphasize. When I put on my business suit for my speeches, it's not just a costume or an outfit. *It's who I am in my business!* I am dressing the part, and I love it! My suits help me take pride in what I do. **Find a look that feels authentic to you and matches your brand, and go all in!**

As far as behavior goes, I believe it is important to stay true to yourself while remaining professional. An unpopular opinion coming in hot... I believe you need to do this at all times. I have a strict policy with my team that when we are running events, they behave appropriately, no matter where they are in the hotel. What I mean is you do not blast loud explicit music in your room, bring girls or guys back to the hotel to sleep around with, or go out and get drunk, and then show up to the hotel ballroom to work the event. Absolutely not. Your behavior needs to be exactly the same when you're working our events as it is when you're in your room with the door locked. It goes a long way, and that's a tough one for many young professionals. We've had to fire many people because their behavior after work didn't match the energy they gave during work. If you are not a positive representation of our brand and culture, it's not a fit. Of course, you can have a drink and enjoy yourself. It's your life. But getting drunk after, during, or before a work event is unacceptable. Period. Showing up late or hungover doesn't fly. It's important to remember these aren't just tips you share with your staff. You have to abide by them, too. I live my life in accordance with what I expect my staff to do. If I don't want them getting sloshed at work, I'm not doing it either. You could run into someone at the car wash, or at the airport, so always look and behave professionally. ***You are representing more than yourself. You are now a brand. People look up to you, so it's vital you understand that responsibility and behave accordingly.***

Whenever you are interacting with someone—it could be a waiter, a stewardess, or your mechanic—make sure you are being kind and treating them the way you would want to be treated. You literally never know who your next customer will be.

Chapter 25
BAD BLOOD

At some point in your small business ownership journey, you will face customers or clients who you literally cannot stand! This is not uncommon, but it is avoidable. Here's how you can avoid picking up clients you despise! Or at least get rid of the bad apples you have in your clientele database.

1. Identify your superpower!
   What is your company's biggest strength? What problems do you love solving? What makes you unique?
2. Who are your favorite clients?
   Literally write them down. Record their names. How did they come to you? How much did they spend with you? Why do you love them? And how did they leave you feeling after working with them?
3. Who are the clients you hate?!
   Again, write it all down. Who are they? How did they come to you? The big issue you face when working with them? How much they spend with you? How you feel after working with them?
4. **Fire all the clients you hate.**
   I mean it! I know you need the business. I know you want the

checks. But they're not healthy for you. Get rid of them. Your team, your business, and you will be better for it! FIRE THEM!
5. Start bringing on new clients who fit the criteria of the clients you LOVE.
When someone comes to do business with you, see if they match your list of favorites. If they do, feel free to bring them on. If not, run away! No one wants bad blood!

When we started using this method, everyone was immediately happier! Our clients were more pleased with the attention and service they were receiving, our staff was grateful to not have to work with people who drained them and left them feeling like shit, *and our profit margins actually improved.* For us, the clients that were a lot of work for us also happened to be the clients who paid us less. The less they paid, the harder they were. They weren't go-getters who made things happen. The clients who paid us the most did the homework we assigned, made stuff happen, and left us feeling energized and invigorated. We were excited to continue the work with them. We couldn't wait for the next call because we knew progress would be made in the time in between. Strange, huh? So we fired all the clients with whom we hated working. We literally refunded their money and told them it wasn't the right fit. And from that point forward, we implemented a strategy that saved us a lot of time, energy, money, and stress. We elected to do pre-interviews before bringing new clients on. We chatted with them about their goals, about their wants, needs and whys, etc. We tried our best to determine if they would be a right fit before we committed. When it came time to discuss payments, we worked solely with those who would pay in full immediately because we'd noticed those who asked for payment plans, or delayed payments, also tended to be hardest to work with. That eliminated quite a few clients. But it saved us, A LOT! And now we have fewer clients who pay us more and who we ADORE working with! It's a win, win, win!

I highly suggest trying this approach with your clients. It can save you a lot of stress, and it can make your team grow stronger in their commitment to you and to your business. It seems scary at first, but in the long run, you'll be thankful you did it! Your staff will be ever so grateful too. I swear it!

Chapter 26
CASH RULES EVERYTHING AROUND ME

When it comes to raising capital for your business, it's important you take a peek into your mindset surrounding money! Some young bosses come from a standpoint of lack, always thinking money is something to be saved and that it takes hard work to get more of it. Whereas others come from an abundance mindset that understands money circulates. Some days you're holding on to it, and other days someone else is, but what goes will always come back. This is how I determine money mindsets around me. Let's say you go grocery shopping and spend $250 on groceries. Some people think, "Dang, that cost me a lot of money. Groceries are expensive. Ughhh, I wish I didn't have to go grocery shopping every week." While others think, "That was a great investment I just made. The $250 I just spent on nutritious food will keep me going all week long. I'm excited to cook and eat this yummy food! What a blessing!"

Now, of course, these are two dramatic approaches, but you understand what I'm saying. Your thoughts about money matter, especially when you are looking to raise capital for your business. **When you go in with a lacking mindset, the investor will feel it.** How are they going to trust you to give them a return on their capital when you don't believe it yourself? You've gotta check yourself! As Kanye West said, "Having money isn't everything. Not having it is." Before you go into a capital-raising conversation, I don't care if your business plan is perfect, your pro forma is unbeatable, you're ready with the Private Placement Memorandum (PPM), you did your research, and you have the perfect investor in front of you. If your mindset isn't right, it won't work.

Many times investors are betting on the jockey and not the horse. Keep that at the forefront of your mind. Why should they invest with YOU and not Joe Schmoe down the road? What makes you special? Why are you the best thing since sliced bread? And if you're not, start your soul searching to determine why you ARE.

For me soul searching begins with knowing yourself. What are your skills? What do you bring to the table? If you cannot think of anything, ask someone close to you—a partner, friend or family member—to list some of the positive attributes they see in you. Try to see what others see inside of you. Sometimes that can spark something! I am not asking you to list 1000 reasons why you're the shit. I'm asking you to **look deep inside and determine who you are, what your skills and strengths are, and play to them**! How can you ask someone to invest in you, trust you, or buy your product if you wouldn't do it yourself? Be the person who you want to invest in, trust, and buy from! Once you know your skills and talents, it's time to position yourself correctly!

Having all of your ducks in a row will also aid in your approach to the investor. You will need a solid business plan. No one wants to see hockey stick projections. Show them reality, which probably looks more like bunny hills. Slowly and steadily increase the profits and be realistic. If the investor is legit, they will be able to smell if you're lying or falsifying the numbers. When it comes to the pro forma and PPM, make sure you're working with a reputable lawyer or business professional to pull together accurate documents, so the prospective investor sees you're serious. One wrong number can sour a deal! I also can't stress enough how important it is to do your research. If this investor is used to deals that are $100 million, don't bring them a $3 million deal. That's not what they do, and you'll likely get turned away. Bring the right deals to the right people. Find out what this particular investor likes to invest in. Do they focus on nonprofits, black-owned businesses, deals under $5 million? What's their preferred type of deal? Find out and then use that research to your advantage. Bring them something that will make sense to them and speak to their preferred investment strategies.

Remember that money is out there! There are tons of people getting about 0 percent return on their money just sitting in the bank, and they are looking for somewhere to invest. We talk about this topic often on the YoungBoss Podcast because it's vital! As a young boss, you may not have the capital to launch your new product or service, and raising capital is something you will probably need to do.

Just remember ***your mindset is everything***. Do your research, have a game plan, get all your documents in a row, be prepared, and GO FOR IT!

Chapter 27
HOW WILL THEY FIND ME?

As a young boss, you cannot underestimate the power of marketing! It's so vital that you literally won't become a powerhouse business without it. Now I know I told you at the beginning of this book that I'm not trying to tell you how to run your business or what to do. I'm just giving you tips and tricks that I've learned along the way. But for real, this is one that everyone—and I mean everyone—I've encountered in business asks me about. How do I market to fill my _____? I always like to think of marketing like this… If I was your customer, how would I search to find out about you? What questions or concerns would I have? What would be the most important things I'm seeking?

For example: if you own a laser hair removal studio, how is someone going to find out about you? More than likely by searching online in their area or asking their friend for a recommendation, right?

- Your website and social media are going to be KEY for your business. Your prospective client needs to be able to see what you do, where you're located, and all the FAQs that might be popping up in their head. Having a strong social media presence with a lot of followers, likes, and reposts will also make them feel more assured about your services.

- When it comes to asking a friend for a recommendation, testimonials are going to help you win over clients, so the more the better. Why should they trust you? Because 1300 other people did! They need proof! Discounts for referrals could be a way to have your clients work for you. If they truly love you, and they're a natural promoter themselves, or are looking to save a few bucks, they'll more than likely take you up on this offer. If you have a client who is an influencer, ask them to partner with you and give them something for free to post about their experience, etc.

Now what concerns would I have as your prospective client? How clean is your facility? Has anyone ever had a bad experience with you? How much will it cost? Am I going to have to show someone 'weird' my private parts to get a laser treatment? Should I trust you? Is this place sketchy?

- The best way to alleviate these concerns is photos and proof! You can post a lot on social media showcasing the office and what it looks like, so the new client knows what to expect.

- You can make funny videos about how it can be uncomfortable or weird to come in for your first time, but reassure them they're in expert hands.

- Introduce yourself and your team. Smiling, beautiful faces make everyone happy!

Lastly, from the prospective customer perspective—what's the last thing that may be holding them back from scheduling with you? It usually comes down to a lack of information. Maybe they don't know when they can book with you, how much it will cost, or how long the appointment will take.

- Again, a nice FAQ page will do the trick for most of those common questions! Answer the questions they haven't even thought of yet! What's aftercare going to be like? What should they avoid, or make sure they do, before they come into your office? What's the cancellation or refund policy?

- A scheduling page that's very easy, or a nice big "contact us" button where they can call to ask questions, will be important.

- Lastly, cost! People don't want to be caught off guard, and you can eliminate a lot of looky-loos by posting your pricing online. The more upfront you are, the better prepared your clients will be walking in the door.

Having a really clean and clear message will help take you to the next level. Always lead with a strong logo and colors that mean something to you. Bring into play your company mission, core values, and culture components. This is your time to shine. The more you show people who you are, the more you attract the right kind of clients. The less upfront you are, the more drama you invite in!

Marketing is what can set you apart from another small business owner. In my industry, Residential Assisted Living, there are a lot of mom-and-pop owners, and nothing against them, but let me tell you—their marketing is WEAK sauce! And it truly rubs off on the clients they are attracting. The websites for our homes are beautiful. They showcase the amenities and features of the homes, they list starting prices, and they have places to see how many open beds we currently have, or if there is a waiting list. The "contact us" is nice and big, and there are a ton of photos, so the prospective seniors can see what their future bedroom, bathroom, living room, kitchen, etc. will look like. Hopefully, it gives them peace of mind! I am proud of the work we have out there and what it's done to expand our business. It's not too flashy. It's not over the top. It's genuine and true to what we offer in the homes, so no one has any indication we are providing something else. It is what it is.

As a young boss, utilize what you know when it comes to marketing. Create a really cool social media presence that can showcase your new business. Make sure it's clean, crisp, and true to your offerings, but don't forget to ask your friends and family and new clients to like, share, and follow. Some people are weird about helping others out in that way, and others will be happy to promote you and your services. And the reality is you've got to start somewhere!

Chapter 28
THE ROLLER COASTER OF PHASES

I think it's important to talk about how a young boss should approach their day-to-day work. This is really important because business has different phases, and you want to make sure you are taking an approach that's suited for each stage of your growth. You have to wear a different set of armor, and prepare for different situations inside and outside of work. If you're in the launch phase, you are just starting. This could last months to years. You are building your business, your clients, your team, and your database. You may have losses because it costs money to run a business, and your capital might not be exceeding your startup costs or loans, etc. If you're in this phase, have fun with it and enjoy the process because it's hard to get out of it. I like to call it 'the grind.' It's important not to overthink. You can get discouraged when sales and numbers aren't where you want them to be. Maybe it's taking longer than you anticipated, but in the end, if you lay the groundwork right, this phase will set you up for more success.

I remember all the fun we had in the launch phase! We were all about building new products and services, and it was the grind of the day-to-day, creating things that people were using and that mattered! It truly is where many entrepreneurs thrive! Most of your energy is used during this phase! Think about a rocket. All the energy is used during takeoff, and then you can start coasting. Well, you will probably never coast in business ownership, but you get what I mean. All the energy is in the beginning, and that's true in business creation as well!

Corporate Finance Institute says, "As sales increase rapidly, businesses start seeing profit once they pass the break-even point. However, as the profit cycle still lags behind the sales cycle, the profit level is not as high as sales. Finally, the cash flow during the growth phase becomes positive, representing excess cash inflow."[5] The growth phase is exactly as it sounds, all about growth! People tend to focus only on cash flow, but this may also be the time your team starts to grow. Maybe you stop working IN your business and start hiring some people to do what you do, so you can delegate and elevate and start working ON your business instead. You have to really step up as a boss in this phase. It's make or break! This phase is also one that doesn't have a strict timeline. You could be in it for a while. It depends on how far and fast you choose to go!

During the growth phase, we looked around and said, "WOW, we really need to start building." This phase comes with some challenges because what got you here won't always get you there! It may be time to look around at some of your people, products or services, and decide that they're phased out. The transition from the launch phase to the growth phase is truly a big one! You've got to stay prepared and vigilant!

At some point, you will hit the shake-out phase. Sales will start to slow down a bit, maybe because of the surrounding market, maybe because of a shift in priorities of people, maybe because of competitors. Whatever the reason, as a young boss, you have to stay prepared and vigilant for this phase because IT WILL COME, and if you don't anticipate it, you may be very disappointed when you hit it. As they say, prepare for the worst; hope for the best. During a shake-out, you may start to panic if your personality doesn't have a high risk

---

5 CFI Team, "Business Life Cycle," CFI, Apr. 26, 2023, https://corporatefinanceinstitute.com/resources/valuation/business-life-cycle/.

tolerance. This could be the phase in which you start taking risks and making moves. If you live in fear of the outcome, this may be a huge challenge for you. Take the Predictive Index quiz to find out how you feel about risk.[6] In my podcast, we talk about the phases of business and how others have approached them. It can be disheartening when you hit your peak, especially if you see it coming. When you see it coming, there are only so many things you can do as a leader in your business. For example, you can make huge adjustments and changes, keep everything the same and pray for the best, or make subtle changes and watch the numbers, productivity, and market closely. Depending on your business, one of those solutions may be an easier or a better choice than the others.

The shake-out phase is not my favorite. It's one of those phases that could be described with the phrase, "When the going gets tough, the tough get going!" You have to be willing to get punched in the gut and jump right back up. In one of our companies, we had a moment where we looked around and said, "I think we are in the shake-out phase." Everyone gulped. That's the energy of this phase. You better pull your boots up and, as a young boss, realize that over everything else, the company comes first. It's your time to make changes that will impact how the rest of your career and business flow! If you don't make a move, the move will be made for you, and you might not be there for the ride. So get ready!

In the fourth phase, maturity, you have some decisions to make, especially if you just sit there and let the shake-out phase happen to you with little to no movement or shifts in your business. In the maturity phase, your sales and numbers are decreasing; you've hit and passed your peak. If you want to last in the long haul, it's time to reinvent yourself, and it's time to reposition. Maturity can be tough to handle depending on how long you've been in the game. If you've been doing

---

6 "Talent Optimization Leader - The Predictive Index," The Predictive Index, accessed Sep. 6, 2023, https://www.predictiveindex.com.

things the exact same way for forty years, and the market has shifted so much that you don't know if you can handle the changes, I get it. It's going to be tough, but this is your make-or-break phase. You have to refresh your growth and jump back to that second phase because, if you don't, you'll head right into the next phase: the dreaded decline.

For us, this time hit during COVID. We are a live seminar business, and all of that was taken from us. We quickly had to revisit how we did things and pivot to survive. We turned all our events virtual, as I know many in business did. Those changes and shifts resulted in ten times our business. We hit our first ever million-dollar weekend, and we did it with ease. We decreased our fifteen-person live team to three people, and we made it happen! We sharpened the tools in the shed, stayed open to feedback, and shifted BIG! We had major concerns, like, *What happens if we don't do it? What if we wait until we are back in person? Will we lose all the down payments for the hotels and take a big financial hit? What if we can't connect with the clients online? What if they don't feel our hearts, our passion, or our love for the seniors and this industry?* But guess what? Staying still and stagnant would have killed us at that moment. Waiting would have led us to shut down. And unfortunately, many businesses did just that. They let fate take control instead of making their own path. No one controls the outcome but you. We refused to let anyone break us, and I hope you are now inspired to do the same!

All companies have to exit some way, somehow. It may be in the decline phase when a company withers away and eventually shuts down, or it could be the decline phase that launches new ideas, new companies, and new businesses. Blockbuster is a prime example of a company in the decline phase—shutting down almost all locations, except one, and accepting their fate. The only way to save yourself from the decline phase is having an exit plan, such as selling the company, leaving the company before the decline phase, or reinvention. If you reinvent, you may save yourself from a true decline phase, and then you can just head back into launch or growth phases. If you started your company with your own two hands, with your own fresh ideas, to watch it go into a decline phase can be very heartbreaking. So be sure that in your business plan, you write out your exit plan. How do you plan to avoid decline? Are you leaving? Or is the company going in another direction? Openness to opportunities can save you from a true decline. If Blockbuster would have jumped at being more of a RedBox type of service, and then eventually becoming the new Netflix, maybe they'd still be around. But instead, they kept doing things the same way, and it led to their eventual fate.

The five phases of business are a nice way to see where you're at and to prepare for what's coming. Sometimes, starting your own business can feel like throwing pasta at the wall and seeing what sticks, and if that's your modus operandi, you're not alone. However, make sure you lay out your business plan at some point. Having a vision and regular goals will keep you on track. If you've never taken the time to write out your business plan or your vision, make sure you connect with an amazing business coach. For me, I love to work with Sharper Business Solutions. Gary and Susan Harper are amazing resources for taking a business from a solopreneur venture to a true, full-throttle company! Nothing lasts forever, but we sure hope your company does!

Chapter 29
RISE

My favorite business coach Gary Harper from Sharper Business Solutions always said, "In order to grow through the five phases of business, you need to mature in resources, inspiration, systems, and engagement." These aspects of your business will help you sustain you long into the future.

1. **R**esources are the tools to help you turn your dreams into reality, which is crucial for any young boss. Dreams can't remain pie in the sky for long. So you need to dedicate time to amassing the resources you need.
2. **I**nspiration needs to come from within. What is going to help you push through the dark times, when no one believes in you? What is that strong why? Write it down, build on it, and lean into it.
3. **S**ystems are critical for success! They will help you save time, energy, and money. If you're a type-A personality like me, you'll want to have them and probably a lot of them. They will ensure things are being done the right way the first time!
4. **E**ngagement is vital—with your team and your clients. What are you doing to get the word out there and stay relevant? Who is listening to you, and what is their feedback? You don't want an audience you just preach to, but you also can't

live in the "comments section." It's that balance of hearing what they are saying and taking it in with a grain of salt!

You must RISE! When it comes to these four major components—building your resources, clarifying your strong why, developing systems, and fostering engagement—the goal is to keep you in this season as long as you can. The YES season. The fun season. The growth season! All of these things will be cyclical. You will continuously do them and improve on them, and that will help you grow. When you are steadily improving, redefining your company purpose, and staying as fresh as possible, you eliminate the quick decline. You can see the future and anticipate things better. My best advice is to stay so fresh, stay so up to date, so innovative, that you really push off decline as long as possible.

Chapter 30
90 PERCENT OF GETTING WHAT YOU WANT...

90 percent of getting what you want is in the presentation. I always share this tactic with my employees and independent contractors because it's so true. If presented correctly, you can get people to give you their money, time, energy, and resources. So work on your presentation and you'll start getting more of what you want, right?! Well, maybe! I like to set my team up for success. I want them to get what they want, and I want to get what I want. So the best way to help us both achieve this goal is to have mutual respect and expectations for the conversation. My four-step process to our meetings helps guide this process, and maybe you'll enjoy it and want to add it to your work practices as well.

1. First, when a manager, director, or anyone in the company comes to our meeting, I let them know the format of the meeting and ask them to be prepared. I want to start the meeting with their wins! This is very important to me because, as a higher-level person in the company, I may not know what they're doing on a day-to-day basis, and for the boss it can feel like no one is doing anything, so I need them

to start with some big wins. What client did they just win over? What meeting did they just crush?

Come with their wins! Let's celebrate them!

2. Next, I need to know what problems they're facing. What is going on for real? This is their chance to get it out. I prefer for my directors and managers to also come with the solutions they've used to solve these issues, but sometimes, they draw a blank. Or, if it's the beginning of our working relationship, they may be hesitant to bring solutions, as they're still learning how I operate. So I'm willing to be impartial on this one for some time based on someone's role in the company. Regardless, this portion of the conversation or meeting is all about issues! We can spend the majority of the time here and work through this until they are feeling better and ready to take on the rest of the day.

3. Third, I want to hear their list of priorities. What do they think is the most important thing they and their team could be working on right now? List it out for me.

4. Lastly, ASK! Ask me if I agree with this priorities list! Because sometimes I may not agree as the boss. I may get frustrated they don't see the importance of certain tasks over others, so this part of the meeting is where we can get in alignment and learn from each other.

If we can follow this four-step meeting process, not only can I see value and be proud of my employees, but I can also feel good about their work and what they are bringing to the table. When I'm 100 percent confident in their list of tasks, I know what's being worked on now and next, and I know they understand why these things are ordered as they are! This method eliminates the guesswork. As an employee, you don't have to wonder what I want done first, if you solved the problem correctly, or if I'm proud of you. You know all these things beyond a shadow of a doubt. The more the team grows and develops, the easier and smoother these meetings get because being on the same page is seamless. I know someone really has transitioned to that other side when their problems and solutions match 90 percent or more with how I would have sorted them out, and their priorities list is in perfect alignment. To be frank, it's never been that way from the get-go. No matter how much you know or like someone, it's impossible to be 100 percent on the same page at first. But over time, these meetings are quick and your team members feel empowered! As we said in the beginning, **90 percent of getting what you want is in the presentation**, so make sure you have discussed the format, everyone is prepared, and you follow the four-step guide. All of these things can aid in your success and, in turn, get you what you want from your team!

Chapter 31
GREED VS SERVITUDE

I want to take a moment to discuss greed in business. Sometimes it's easy to get caught up in the money to be made, in the cash flow that starts coming in, in the success, in your ideas coming to fruition… but the reality is you can never ever, ever let greed overcome service. When you are presenting a deal or opportunity to someone, don't forget it's about the story. It's about how you can serve them, NOT how much money you can make! It's NOT about you, AT ALL! It has to be a trust-building moment where you are presenting the opportunity to change lives. If a guy walks into a bar and wants something for the night, he behaves a certain way—but if he wants something for a lifetime, he behaves differently. That's what I'm referring to. Don't be in this for the money, or for whatever you can get out of it. Be in this for the betterment of our world, this person, your client, whomever it is. If it's all about you or the money to be made, that will show through. "Give three times and ask once" is a good rule to live by. When you *focus on relational success over transactional success*, you win. People want to connect with people, with businesses that have authenticity and a positive association attached to them. Your branding should speak for itself.

Chapter 32
SHINY PENNY SYNDROME

I have had a unique experience in my career, being in both the Integrator position as well as the Visionary position. This is not common, as most people's brains work one way or the other and are not able to truly switch and thrive in both of these modes. But because of this unique experience and ability, I have a strong understanding of what it takes from both sides. If you are the Visionary of your company, this may be a nice section to share with your right hand, your Integrator, to give them some insight into your brain and the way you think.

A NOTE TO INTEGRATORS:

When it comes to being focused in business, it's really important to think about shiny penny syndrome. Visionaries have a lot of ideas! They are, as I like to call them, a broken fire hydrant! They spout off ideas and let them fall where they may! The Integrator's role is never to tell the Visionary no, but instead how to make those ideas reality. For example, when my dad was our company's Visionary, he would give me three new product ideas and five new business ideas, almost weekly! What can I say? He was creative! And let me tell you—these weren't small ventures. He would want to start a TV show, a podcast, write a book series, launch an app, and rewrite our curriculum, while creating a new seminar on public speaking and pitching to investors, all in one week! Mind you, I was already running eight companies and a team of fifty employees. Visionaries are all gas, as they say. Now these were amazing ideas. I understood why he wanted to do them and what he saw in them, but we couldn't do everything at once. This was where shiny penny syndrome came in, because sometimes he would hang with other entrepreneurs and get excited about what they were doing and want to do it too. Or see something on TV, or hear something on a podcast, and think, "Hey, we could do that too!" So as his Integrator, it was my role to flesh them all out: what would it look like to get there, how much it would cost us, who needed to be involved, what could go wrong, and how it would affect the other businesses. Most importantly, I would have to ask why he wanted to do it in the first place. I would extract all the information I could from him about the idea, asking curious questions and giving him direct responses, because let's be real—most Visionaries haven't really thought through their ideas when they bring them to the table. They're just dreams and ideas! A Visionary's superpower doesn't lie in the details. It lies in creativity. Once I had a concept I could work with, I would pull together a business plan with all those details and present it back to him. In turn, he would say yes or no, and then we'd move forward. If a no, the smartest thing an Integrator can do is retain the business plan and idea somewhere. That way you can refer back to the plan, and why they vetoed it, if they bring it up again down the line. Maybe when it resurfaces, they've sorted out the challenge, or maybe you need to remind them why they said no in the first place. They may be the gas, but you are the brakes.

Now if they say maybe later, do the same thing. Take all the notes and put them away for a later date. Remind yourself to follow up with them on it, and go forward from there. If it's a yes, this is your chance to impress them. Ask any clarifying questions you may have regarding the plan you've laid out and get prepared to implement it with your team. You'll need to be able to answer all the questions—why, when, where, and how this is happening. Your job is to keep your Visionary and your team focused on this project, and all the other ones going on. Knowing everyone's capacity is key because that helps you determine what more they can put on their plates versus who you'll have to hire to bring this new idea to life.

NOW, TO MY VISIONARIES:

Now that your Integrator understands you a little bit more, let's get back to you. When it comes to your fresh ideas, this is where you shine! I never want anyone to dull your sparkle and make you feel like they're always telling you NO! That's never fun, and in your world, you thrive on "let's get it done" attitudes. Keep in mind: your Integrator is not telling you no. They're trying to protect you and keep you focused. It's the balance of the gas and brakes. We can't have one or the other! When you stay focused on the task, project, and company at hand, you can excel and make your dreams a reality. When you jump around and have shiny penny syndrome, you can get lost, and nothing ever gets brought to fruition or fully executed. That balance of the how and the excitement is why you chose this person for your right-hand woman or man! They know what to do to make sure you're going to succeed. Being involved in a lot of creative environments like masterminds and groups of entrepreneurs can stimulate lots of new ideas, but it can also be a detriment to you. So protect yourself or, at least, rely on your Integrator to protect you. If you feel strongly about something, it's okay to push for it, but make sure you have everyone on board. Too often we see Integrators overwhelmed by the Visionary's propensity for distraction, and the Visionary is furious about the fact that the Integrator isn't more enthusiastic about their ideas. **Balance is key. Communication is key. Focus is key.** Follow one course until you're successful. Do what you need to do to see it to fruition! You can jump around and have a lot of different things going at once as long as your Integrator is implementing. After all, Richard Branson has over 800 companies. Do you think he knows what's happening in all of them? Probably not, and that's okay. He's living in his superpower, creation/idea generation and inspiration! If that's you, build yourself a team with Integrators who get it and are ready to move to the next level with you!

Chapter 33
WE'RE ALL IN THIS TOGETHER—OR ARE WE?!

On the YoungBoss Podcast, I get to have incredible conversations with other entrepreneurs and business owners. It's there I noticed a trend. It seems many small business owners date/marry/get engaged to other small business owners and even end up working together. Now, I love working with friends and family, and I have worked with my ex-husband, but I know it's not for everyone. And no, that's not why we got divorced. HA! Personally, I've noticed it takes three traits to make it work at work with your partner.

1. You must be willing to waffle!
   Remember that old phrase, women are spaghetti brains, and men are waffle brains? If you're going to work with your partner, you've got to learn to have a waffle brain! You have to compartmentalize your life and your work. If you don't, you will inevitably start to resent your partner for something that you did in the other environment, and it will lead to fights. That's not what I, nor you, want! You must stop the mush! You must cease the spaghetti brain! Stop letting things affect other things. The truth is, in most cases, they don't! And if they do, and you really can't get over it, then you shouldn't work with

your partner because it's not worth losing someone you love over a business. ***The bedroom is not the boardroom. Keep them separate!***

2. Live in gratitude
   Play to each other's strengths and learn one another's weaknesses! For me, this is a great way to strengthen your work and home life. The more you learn about one another in and out of work, the better. You will grow in admiration and respect for what the other brings to the table. One of my great friends used to work with his wife, and he said, "You know, she's so good at the initial meetings with the clients. She wins them all! I'm too shy. Sometimes clients don't connect with me right at the start, but when it comes to the paperwork, I am the king!" So they built a system where she dealt with all the new clients and locked down the contracts while he dealt with all the back-end paperwork. They both got to do what they loved and live in their strengths. This is a great way to look at one another as assets instead of annoyances. Your partner is not you, and you are not them, but this is a good thing. ***Live in gratitude. Live in a place of knowing and thankfulness for what they DO bring to the table.*** Balance is what makes the world go round after all!

3. Honesty is the best policy
   There are going to be tough conversations you'll need to have if you choose to work with your partner. And guess what? You're not going to want to have them. Maybe one of your employees felt weird about an interaction with your partner, and they came to you to share it. Guess what? You have to say something! Or maybe they are dressed like a slob kabob, and it's not appropriate, and you're going to have to be the one to break

the news—they need a new wardrobe. Or, if they were wrong on a number in a meeting, or if they asked if they were too harsh during the firing call, and… they were! Those are situations in which you will probably have to lead with honesty. While you don't have to be rude about it, you do have to tell the truth. Hard conversations breed trust when dealt with correctly. **You can't be scared about repercussions. Sometimes you have to put on the hat of knowing where, when, and how to deliver those harsh truths.** Still, that's the same hat you'd put on with any tough conversation with your team members. Treat them with the same tact. Don't hit them upside the head with the terrible things they did that week, but also don't shy away from telling them the truth about their shortcomings. Be real! You'll never lose if you stay in the honest zone.

Working with a partner can be similar to working with a friend or family member, and that I also know all too well! I love working with my family and friends. Residential Assisted Living Academy was started by my late father Gene Guarino, and I now run the business with my mother, my sister, and my youngest brother. Over the years, my cousins, my uncles, my sister-in-law, brother-in-law, another brother, friends, ex-mother-in-law, and many more worked for us! I've learned quite a few lessons, but honestly, they all boil down to one. For some, it's never going to work. Either you can't hold them to the same standards, or you can't be honest with yourself or them about their performance, effort, or output.

Remember when we talked about firing people? It sucks! But with partners and family members, it's even worse!!! For others, it's the best situation possible. I know in each of my relationships with my family members, it took a special conversation about what it would look like to work together and, more importantly, what it would look like if we ever stopped. You see, sometimes, it's not going to be a choice.

Sometimes, you're going to want them to leave, and other times, they're going to want to leave, or others are going to want them to leave. You need to be prepared for all of those scenarios. As a young boss, I highly suggest you have this conversation before hiring them. Let them know it's business, not personal, and you want to maintain a solid relationship with them post-working together. This conversation could save your relationships! Seriously! Don't skip it! It's like getting a prenup. You wanna have the conversation when you're still in a good place, so that when things aren't, you have everything laid out on the table.

I love working with friends and family. One of the benefits and perks is being able to merge work and life. I get to spend built-in quality time with my siblings. When I come into the office, we talk about their kids, their partners, their life, and work in one conversation. When I chat with my employees who are friends, we schedule a meeting and our next cycle class in the same breath. I love it! There's nothing like it! I enjoy spending time with all of them. I look forward to our meetings because I get to check in on them and hear about their days. Work doesn't feel like work because it's fun! Truly, I feel like the luckiest, most blessed girl on Planet Earth because of my incredible team, many of whom started as strangers and became wonderful friends. Work and life can successfully overlap, and it's a lot easier when the people you work with are the people you do life with. I know it's not for everyone, but if you're not going to work with friends and family, who does that leave you with? Enemies and strangers!? No, thank you! Not for me!

Chapter 34
STICKY STICKY

I want to address two really difficult things in leadership roles many young bosses will face. The first is leading someone who is older than you! This can be very challenging, depending on this person's experience in the industry or field, and how they feel about you having that position of esteem. I remember a time when my boss was choosing between myself and someone else for a leadership role. The other candidate was about fifty-five years old, and I was around twenty-four. The boss chose me. The other candidate still had to work with me. I was their director. Suffice to say, they were not happy about it, and they definitely made it known. They opposed everything I said or tried to implement and tried to turn other coworkers against me. After six months of this back-and-forth, I'd had enough. I eventually took my coworker into a small private room and said, "You know, I get it. You wanted this role and didn't get it. I did. Maybe you deserved it with your experience, but the reality is the boss chose me. So either you get on board and stop trying to undermine everything I do, or you can leave this company. It's up to you. What I will not allow is bad behavior. Are you here for the company or for yourself? What's the decision?"

The other employee was triggered, but he understood I was telling him the truth. He put down his weapons and said, "I am on the team, and I want to be here. I will work harder, and together, instead of opposing you." That was the end of it. I'm not saying I handled it perfectly, but I was direct. It left very little room for misinterpretation. I tried to have a friendly conversation with him. I tried to ask my boss for support. Nothing was working, and it was making me regret taking the leadership position. Not only did I love this company, but I loved my new role, and I wasn't going to let one person take it from me.

We all know that one Karen in the office who can't help but remind us how little experience we have or how young and precious we are. Guess what, Karen?! **Youth is our power.** We deserve a spot in the workplace just like you did when you were our age, and just like you do now. We both deserve to be here. And that's that!

Don't let others look down on you because you are young. There is a different way to handle every generation, sex, and personality type, and you're not going to do it perfectly, but if you treat others the way you want to be treated, you're going to be more than okay! Being young in business is not something to be ashamed of. It's not something to be looked down upon. It's your power. Live in it! Be proud of yourself and how far you've come! You deserve that leadership role, and no one should make you feel otherwise.

Now the other very sticky situation that's hard to deal with in business relationships is being a boss to someone who used to be a coworker. This one is tricky because they often have a hard time viewing you as their boss. You go from goofing off with someone, to being responsible for their output and productivity, and your silly attitude and jovial spirit have to transition into something a bit harsher. It's hard for both people, but especially hard to be the boss because you feel like you're losing a friend. You may lose friends. People may start to tease you and call you names. This can deter some people from taking leadership roles, but to me, it sounds like a bunch of crabs. These types of people want to pull you down because you're trying to get out of the bucket. Don't let their jokes bother you. The truth is you CAN remain friends with someone you now lead. You have to go about it all in the right way, being mindful and kind and remembering what it was like to be in their position. When you adopt this attitude, you can make the best of the changed situation, continuing your friendship while expecting the best of them as your subordinate.

Chapter 35
FORECASTING

For most entrepreneurs, it's hard to see the end of anything. We like to ride the wave and don't prepare for the exit very well. I can relate. I love what I do and want to keep teaching and training on Residential Assisted Living until the wheels fall off. At the same time, I want to make sure I get out on top, whatever that may look like. The last thing I want is to have worked ten to fifteen years on building a huge business and let it all fall apart in the end. I would much rather sell the company and be a sideline cheerleader for the next leader who takes over. I'm not sure what direction we will go, but I pray I don't have to watch it all crumble. Although I can't anticipate everything, this is my goal for RAL Academy and the other Impact Housing Group companies.

The good thing is I know I'm living my dream life. I love my team. I am blessed to be surrounded by the most incredible coworkers and employees I could ask for. I am thrilled to work in an industry that is fulfilling to me, a place where I can see my teachings make a huge impact on people's lives. I have the joy of working with family and friends, and I want to bring everyone with me along for the ride. Every single day, I get to connect with other inspiring business owners and hear about what works and doesn't work and what I should watch out for. It's the most exhilarating and dynamic thing I have ever done, and the truth is… I didn't set out to do it. I kind of got pushed into it, as you heard in the beginning, but I am so elated for what the future holds. I found my WHY, my legacy, and I am honored to guide my team day-by-day in the best adventure I've ever been on.

I don't see myself ever working for the man now. Never say never, but now that I've gotten a taste of being my own boss, it just doesn't sound appealing to go backwards. If the world stops and everything gets taken from me, I would more than likely just pick myself up by my bootstraps and restart. I would hire most of the same people since I know, trust, and love them and attempt to do it all again. Perhaps I'd do it in the same field since I adore working in senior housing and know the industry so well, but I might look to try it in another field. All I know for certain is I don't want this journey to end. I refuse to be disappointed by the person I've become. I want to give this day, and every day, my all.

When it comes to the YoungBoss Podcast, I am so excited for what the future holds. I started this community to curate a space for other entrepreneurs to be challenged, understood, and heard. We are the minority, and we need representation. I wondered why there wasn't as much in the marketplace, and then I realized the statistics and said to myself, *Well, why not me? Why can't I be the one to create the room and see who walks in?* The YoungBoss Podcast has been an incredible outlet for me to share my thoughts and learned lessons about being a young entrepreneur, and it's been an invaluable resource for me to connect with others in many different fields about their wins and struggles. **Being an entrepreneur can be a lonely journey, and it can be hard or embarrassing to talk about the things that fluster you in this solo world.** For me it's been edifying to lay my failures on the table for the world to see—like bringing on a bad hire, totally missing the sales quota, not hitting the mark on a vital presentation, disappointing a client, getting an egg. These are all topics we discuss on the podcast. If you haven't listened and are intrigued by what we've been discussing here in this book, feel free to check it out at https://theyoungbosspodcast.com. It may just be the source of knowledge, insight, and connection you've been seeking. Make sure to share any impactful episodes with your other young boss friends, too. I want to see the community grow and create a space for just us!

Being a young boss is many things. It's hard. It's fun. It's heartbreaking. It's exhilarating. It's challenging. It's crucial to your growth. It's all of these things and more. I am blessed to be in the 6 percent of young bosses, and hopefully, you are too or soon will be! Let's ride this thing until the wheels fall off and then get back up and rebuild. You're smart. You're motivated. You're a young boss. Welcome to the YB family!

TOP TIPS FOR YOUNG BOSSES

1. You have to let things go.
2. Your way is not always the best way.
3. Do what it takes to get the job done, no matter what.
4. You have to know your strengths and play to them.
5. Choose the company first. Be predictable with your actions.
6. Show them what work-life balance looks like, not by faking it, but really, truly doing it.
7. It's not enough to create the vision and let it sit there. You must actively read it. You must attach emotions and feelings to it.
8. Start where you are. Use what you have. Begin today!
9. Being a leader will bring out many different sides of you, and it will push you to new limits you never knew existed.
10. There is power in saying no.
11. If you don't know how to do something, become an expert, then come back and tackle it.
12. Being a solopreneur is a lot of fun because there is no one you have to answer to or be responsible for, and you get to make every single decision on your own. Do what works for you!
13. If you've done it once, you can do it again.

14. It's not about you as an entrepreneur or business owner; it's actually about everyone else.
15. You have to be willing to get punched in the face and get back up over and over again.
16. Change your perspective and save your life.
17. Categorize your friendships and try to find a tribe who can relate to you.
18. Having a team, a group of people you can call on, makes life worth living. It helps you excel. It helps push you.
19. Take what you need and give what you can.
20. You must be IN the moment when you're celebrating!
21. Oftentimes, your team will have excellent insight into matters that you don't see or understand yet.
22. Listen to your competition.
23. When you enter a room and you're humble, sharing both your successes and failures, people see an authentic soul, and they want to reach out for feedback, networking, and connections.
24. Staying humble will literally help you do things faster and better. It will also leave room for more financial opportunities.
25. Being fired sucks. And firing someone sucks, too! Stay calm, be kind, and remember that at one point, you were stoked to hire this person.
26. If they are thinking about leaving, let them go. They'll be happier elsewhere, and you'll be happier not stressing about their happiness or fulfillment at your company.
27. One wrong hire can cost you a lot of money, time, resources, and stress.
28. It's much easier to train someone by showing them, than to explain to them.

29. We spend most of our days and time at work. It should be a place we enjoy.
30. When you're in a male-dominated field, it's okay to put your masculine energy forward and first. You have to be strong and domineering, and you can't take no for an answer.
31. We women are the underdogs, and we have the strength and power to say, "I get it, and I'm ready to work ten times harder. No challenge is too big."
32. Running a business is the ONLY way to play in the game of life. This is the best way to control your income, live to your true potential, and become the highest and best version of yourself.
33. Find a look that feels authentic to you and matches your brand, and go all in!
34. You are representing more than yourself. You are now a brand. People look up to you, so it's vital you understand that responsibility and behave accordingly.
35. Fire all the clients you hate.
36. When you go in with a lacking mindset, the investor will feel it.
37. Look deep inside and determine who you are, what your skills and strengths are, and play to them!
38. Your mindset is everything.
39. Having a really clean and clear message is what makes marketing help you take your company to the next level.
40. All companies have to exit some way, somehow.
41. 90 percent of getting what you want is in the presentation.
42. Focus on relational success over transactional success.
43. Balance is key. Communication is key. Focus is key.
44. The bedroom is not the boardroom. Keep them separate!
45. Live in gratitude. Live in a place of knowing and thankfulness for what your people DO bring to the table.

46. You can't be scared about repercussions. Sometimes you have to put on the hat of knowing where, when, and how to deliver those harsh truths.
47. Youth is our power.

AUTHOR BIO

Isabelle Guarino is the COO of Impact Housing Group. She trains and coaches entrepreneurs and investors at the Residential Assisted Living Academy. With a background in Business Marketing and Communications, from interning at Walt Disney World to working at two Fortune 500 companies, she is a true leader in business development and operations. She is responsible for the creation and success of RAL National Convention, RAL National Association, Recovery Housing Academy, Pitch Masters Academy, and most of the Impact Housing Group's companies.

Isabelle has spoken across the country and has been featured in magazines and articles nationally. She was named a "Future Leader" in the Senior Housing industry and a "Top Senior Housing Influencer" under 30, as well as one of the "Top 5 Disruptive Entrepreneurs Going Into 2023."

Isabelle is an Amazon best-selling author of the book *Living Legacy* and the host of the YoungBoss Podcast! The YB podcast is a place for young bosses and entrepreneurs of all industries to collaborate and chat about the expected (and unexpected) challenges of being a successful, young professional in today's business environment. With weekly Wednesday episodes on discussions about leadership, personal growth, networking and building relationships, raising capital, business strategy, and SO much more!

Isabelle is a sought-after coach and trainer for all things "RAL!" Isabelle's mission is to positively impact 10,000,000 people through Residential Assisted Living and carry on her father's legacy by training investors and entrepreneurs how to "Do Good & Do Well," especially Young Bosses.

www.ingramcontent.com/pod-product-compliance
Lightning Source LLC
Chambersburg PA
CBHW052221090526
44585CB00015BA/1265